The Religions of the Ancient World

By

George Rawlinson

Published by Forgotten Books 2012

Originally Published 1883

PIBN 1000073956

THE RELIGIONS

OF

THE ANCIENT WORLD,

INCLUDING

EGYPT,	PHŒNICIA,
ASSYRIA AND BABYLONIA,	ETRURIA,
PERSIA,	GREECE,
INDIA,	ROME.

BY

GEORGE RAWLINSON, M. A.,

CAMDEN PROFESSOR OF ANCIENT HISTORY, OXFORD,
AND CANON OF CANTERBURY;

Author of " The Origin of Nations," " The Five Great Monarchies " etc.

NEW YORK

CHARLES SCRIBNER'S SONS

1883

GRANT, FAIRES & RODGERS, PRINTERS

52 & 54 NORTH SIXTH STREET

PHILADELPHIA

PREFACE.

This little work has originated in a series of papers written for the *Sunday at Home* in the years 1879 and 1881, based upon Lectures delivered in the University of Oxford, from the chair which I have the honour to hold. During the twenty-one years that I have occupied that chair, I have continually felt more and more that the real history of nations is bound up with the history of their religions, and that, unless these are carefully studied and accurately known, the inner life of nations is not apprehended, nor is their history understood.

I have also felt that the desire to generalize upon the subject of ancient religions, and to build up a formal "Science of Religion," as it is called, has outrun the necessarily anterior collection of materials on which generalization might be safely based. I have, therefore, in my lectures to students, made a point of drawing their attention, from time to time, to the religious beliefs and practices of the various races and nations with whom my historical teaching has been concerned, and of exhibiting to them, as well as I was able, at once the external features and the internal characteristics of "The Religions of the Ancient World."

But the voice of a Professor, speaking *ex cathedrâ* rarely reaches far, nor do modern academical reforms tend in the direction of enlarging professorial influence within Universities. It thus becomes necessary for Professors, if they wish to advance the studies in which they feel especial interest, to address the world without through the Press, and this I have accordingly done from time to time, and shall probably continue to do, while life and strength are granted to me.

Of the shortcomings of the present work no one can be more conscious than its author. I have represented myself towards its close (p. 239) as having done no more than touched the fringe of a great subject. Should circumstances permit, and sufficient encouragement be received, the sketch of Ancient Religions here put forth may not improbably receive at some future time such an expansion as may render it more proportionate to the vast matter of which it treats.

It is impossible to make acknowledgments to all those whose works I have consulted with advantage. But my obligations to Professor Max Müller's dissertations upon the Vedas, to Dr. Martin Haug's "Essays on the Parsee Religion," and to Mr. Dennis's "Cities and Cemeteries of Etruria" seem to require special recognition. Apart from the works of these writers, three of the "Religions" could not have been so much as attempted. If I have ventured sometimes, though rarely, to differ from their conclusions, it has been with diffidence and reluctance.

CONTENTS.

INTRODUCTION.

CHAPTER I.

The Religion of the Ancient Egyptians.

CHAPTER II.

The Religion of the Assyrians and Babylonians.

CHAPTER III.

The Religion of the Ancient Iranians.

CHAPTER IV.

The Religion of the Early Sanskritic Indians.

CHAPTER V.

The Religion of the Phœnicians and Carthaginians.

CHAPTER VI.

THE RELIGION OF THE ETRUSCANS.

CHAPTER VII.

THE RELIGION OF THE ANCIENT GREEKS.

CHAPTER VIII.

THE RELIGION OF THE ANCIENT ROMANS.

CONCLUDING REMARKS.

LIST OF ILLUSTRATIONS.

THE RELIGIONS

OF

THE ANCIENT WORLD.

INTRODUCTION.

"Religio est, quæ superioris cujusdam, naturæ, quam Divinam vocant, curam cærimoniamque affert."—CIC. *De Inventione*, ii. 53.

IT is the fashion of the day to speculate on the origins of things. Not content with observing the mechanism of the heavens, astronomers discuss the formation of the material universe, and seek in the phenomena which constitute the subject-matter of their science for "Vestiges of Creation." Natural philosophers propound theories of the "Origin of Species," and the primitive condition of man. Comparative philologists are no longer satisfied to dissect languages, compare roots, or contrast systems of grammar, but regard it as incumbent upon them to put forward views respecting the first beginnings of language itself.

To deal with facts is thought to be a humdrum

1

and commonplace employment of the intellect, one
fitted for the dull ages when men were content to
plod, and when progress, development, "the higher
criticism" were unknown. The intellect now takes
loftier flights. Conjecture is found to be more
amusing than induction, and an ingenious hypothesis
to be more attractive than a proved law. Our "advanced thinkers" advance to the furthest limits of
human knowledge, sometimes even beyond them;
and bewitch us with speculations, which are as beautiful, and as unsubstantial, as the bubbles which a
child produces with a little soap and water and a
tobacco-pipe.

Nor does even religion escape. The historical
method of inquiry into the past facts of religion is in
danger of being superseded by speculations concerning what is called its "philosophy," or its "science."
We are continually invited to accept the views of
this or that theorist respecting the origin of all religions, which are attributed either to a common innate idea or instinct, or else to a common mode of
reasoning upon the phenomena and experiences of
human life. While the facts of ancient religions are
only just emerging from the profound obscurity that
has hitherto rested upon them, fancy is busy con-
structing schemes and systems, which have about as
much reality as the imaginations of a novelist or the
day-dreams of an Almaschar. The patient toil, the
careful investigation which real Science requires as
the necessary basis upon which generalisation must
proceed, and systems be built up, is discarded for

the "short and easy method" of jumping to conclusions and laying down as certainties what are, at the best, "guesses at truth."

It is not the aim of the present writer to produce a "Science of Religion," or even to speculate on the possibility of such a science being ultimately elaborated when all the facts are fully known. He has set himself a more prosaic and less ambitious task— that, namely, of collecting materials which may serve as a portion of the data, when the time comes, if it ever comes, for the construction of the science in question. A building cannot be erected without materials; a true science cannot be constructed without ample data.

Careful inquiries into the real nature of historical religions are necessary preliminaries to the formation of any general theories on the subject of religion worth the paper upon which they are written. And such inquiries have, moreover, a value in themselves. "The proper study of mankind is man;" and the past history of the human race possesses an undying interest for the greater portion of educated human kind. Of that past history there is no branch more instructive, and few more entertaining, than that which deals with religious beliefs, opinions, and practices. Religion is the most important element in the thought of a nation; and it is by studying their religions that we obtain the best clue to the inner life and true character of the various peoples who have played an important part in the drama of human affairs.

In the ensuing pages the religious tenets and practices of eight principal nations of antiquity are passed in review—the nations being those with which ancient history is chiefly concerned—the Egyptians, Assyrians and Babylonians, Iranians, Sanskritic Indians, Phœnicians, Etruscans, Greeks, and Romans.

The religion of the Jews has been omitted, as sufficiently well known to all educated persons. The religions of ancient barbarous races have been excluded, as not having come down to us in any detail, or upon sufficiently trustworthy evidence. The eight nations selected have, on the contrary, left monuments and writings, more or less extensive, from which it has seemed to be possible to give a tolerably full account of their religious beliefs, and one on which a fair degree of dependence may be placed. No doubt, as time goes on, and fresh discoveries are made of ancient documents, or an increased insight obtained into the true meaning of their contents, we shall come to know much more than we know at present on the subject here handled; but it is confidently believed that further research and study will only supplement, and not contradict, the views which are here put forward. The author will gladly see the sketch which he here attempts filled up and completed by others. Δόξειεν ἂν παντὸς εἰναι προαγαγεῖν καὶ διαρθρῶσαι τὰ καλῶς ἔχοντα τῇ περιγραφῃ, καὶ ὁ χρόνος των τοιουτων ευρετης, ἡ συνεργὸς ἀγαθὸς εἶναι. ὅθεν καὶ τῶν τεχνῶν γεγόνασιν επιδόσεις· παντὸς γαρ προσθεῖναι το ελλεῖπον.

CHAPTER I.

THE RELIGION OF THE ANCIENT EGYPTIANS.

Αἰγύπτιοι . . . θεοσιβέες περισσῶς ἐόντες μάλιστα πάντων
ανθρωπων.—HEROD. ii. 37.

THE religions of the ancient world, if we except Judaism, seem to have been, all of them,
more or less polytheistic ; but the polytheism grew
up in different ways, was carried out to very different
lengths, and proceeded upon considerably varying
principles. In some places natural objects and operations appear to have presented themselves to the un-
sophisticated mind of man as mysterious, wonderful,
divine ; and light, fire, the air, the sun, the moon,
the dawn, the cloud, the stream, the storm, the lightning, drew his attention separately and distinctly,
each having qualities at which he marvelled, each, as
he thought, instinct with life, and each, therefore,
regarded as a Power, a Being—the natural and
proper object of worship and reverence. Elsewhere,
men seem to have begun with a dim and faint appreciation of a single mysterious power in the world
without them, and to have gradually divided this
power up into its various manifestations, which by
degrees became separate and distinct beings. The

5

process in this case might stop short after a few steps had been taken, or it might be carried on almost interminably, until a pantheon had been formed in which the mind lost itself.

Where the polytheism grew up out of an analysis, the principle of the division might be either physical or metaphysical ; a separation of nature into its parts, or an analysis of the Being presiding over nature into his various powers and attributes. Or these two processes might be combined and intermixed, the pantheon being thus still further enlarged at the expense of some confusion of thought and complexity of arrangement. Again, occasionally, there was a further enlargement and complication, in consequence of the desire to embrace in one system analyses which were really distinct, or to comprise in a single national religion local diversities of arrangement or nomenclature, or even to admit into a system based on one principle elements which belonged properly to systems based upon others. The whole result in such a case was one of extensive complexity, and even contradiction ; a tangle was produced which it was scarcely possible to unravel. The system, however, gained in richness and variety what it lost in logical sequence and intelligibility, and continued to have a firm hold on the minds of many when religions of greater internal consistency had lost their power.

The Egyptian polytheism was of the character last described. Its most striking characteristics were its multitudinousness, its complexity, and the connection of this latter feature with early local diversities in the names and offices of the gods. Wilkinson, who does not profess to exhaust the subject, enumerates seventy-three divinities, and gives their several names and forms.[1] Birch has a list of sixty-three "*principal* deities,"[2] and notes that "others personified the elements, or presided over the operations of nature, the seasons, and events."[3] It is not, perhaps, too much to say, that the Egyptian pantheon in its final form comprised some hundreds of gods and goddesses,[4] each known under a different name, and each discharging more or less peculiar functions. We say, "each discharging more or less peculiar functions," since some deities were so nearly alike, came so close the one to the other, that their identity or diversity is a moot point, still disputed among Egyptologists. In other cases the diversity is greater, yet still the features possessed in common are so numerous that the gods can scarcely be considered wholly distinct, and, indeed, are not unfrequently confounded together and blended into ·a single personage. We hear of Amen-Ra, Amen-Kneph, Ra-Harmachis, Isis-Selk, Phthah-Sokari-Osiris, and the like. There is reason to believe that

[1] "Manners and Customs of the Ancient Egyptians," vols. iv. and v. For the forms, see his "Supplement," plates 21 to 72.

[2] See his "Dictionary of Hieroglyphics" in Bunsen's "Egypt," vol. v. pp. 581–583.

[3] "Guide to the British Museum," p. 4.

[4] An inscription of Rameses II. speaks of "the *thousand* gods, the gods male, the gods female, those which are of the land of Egypt" ("Records of the Past," vol. iv. p. 31); but this phrase is no doubt rhetorical.

a main cause of this multiplication of deities, nearly or quite the same, which at first sight seems so strange and unaccountable, is to be found in the originally local character of many of the gods, and the subsequent admission of purely provincial deities into the general pantheon.

With a view to educe order out of this multitudinous confusion, attempts were made by the Greeks, and perhaps by some of the later Egyptians themselves, to classify the deities, and divide them into certain ranks or orders, each of which should comprise a certain definite number. Herodotus speaks of a first, a second, and a third order,[1] and assigns positively to the first order eight, and to the second twelve gods, leaving the third rank indeterminate. Some traces of a similar classification are found in some of the native writers;[2] and it is generally agreed that a distinction of ranks was recognized; but when an endeavor is made to specify the gods of each rank, insurmountable difficulties present themselves. It seems clear that even the first eight gods were not established by the general consent of the nation in all parts of Egypt, and probable that in one and the same place they were not always the same at different periods. According to what seems the earliest tradition, the eight names were those of Phthah, Ra, Shu (or Kneph),[3] Seb, Osiris, Isis, Set,

[1] Herod. ii. 43.

[2] As Manetho (ap. Euseb. "Chron. Can." i. 19).

[3] The name given is Agathodæmon, who is thought to represent one or other of these gods.

and Horus; according to the latest researches, they were, at Memphis, Phthah, Shu, Tefnu, Seb, Nu (or Nut), Osiris, Isis, and Athor; while at Thebes they were Ammon, Mentu, Tum (or Atum), Shu, Seb, Osiris, Set, and Horus.[1] Others have thought to find them in Ammon, Khem, Maut, Kneph, Sati, Phthah, Neith, and Ra,[2] or in this list with a single change—that of the last name, for which it is proposed to substitute that of Bast or Pasht.[3] It is evident that, while the chief authorities are thus at variance, no certain list of even the eight great gods can be put forward.

The twelve gods of the second order are still more indeterminate. Two lists have been formulated, one by Sir G. Wilkinson, and the other by the late Baron Bunsen, but each includes three deities which are excluded by the other.[4] The formation of such lists

---

[1] See Birch's "Egypt from the Earliest Times to B.C. 300," " Introduction," pp. x. xi., and compare "Guide to the British Museum," p. 12.

[2] Bunsen's "Egypt's Place in Ancient History," vol. i. pp. 366–367.

[3] Wilkinson, in Rawlinson's "Herodotus," vol. ii. pp. 284-286 (32nd edition).

[4] Bunsen's list consists of—

Chons	*Bast	*Ma	Savak
Thoth	*Athor	Tafné	Seb
Tum	Shu	Mentu	Netpe;

Wilkinson's of—

*Ra	Khons	Shu	Savak
Seb	*Anouke	Tafné	*Seneb
Netpe	Tum	Thoth	Mentu

The peculiar names are marked with an asterisk.

is mere guess-work; and the conclusion to be drawn from the attempts made is that, while the Egyptians recognised a gradation of ranks among their deities, and assigned to some a position of decided superiority, to others one, comparatively speaking, inferior, there was no "hard-and-fast line" separating rank from rank, or order from order, nor was any definite number of divinities reckoned in any division.

Still, we can easily particularise the principal divinities, the gods which were the chief objects of worship, either in the main centres of population, or throughout the country. There can be no doubt that to this class belong Ammon, Khem, Kneph, Phthah, Ra, Osiris, and Neith. Ammon was the chief god of Thebes, Khem of Chemmis, or Panopolis, Kneph of Elephantine, Phthah of Memphis, Ra of Heliopolis, Osiris of Abydos and Philæ, Neith of Sais. It will perhaps be a better illustration of the Egyptian religion to give a particular though brief account of these seven deities than to waste pages in generalities.

Ammon is said to have meant, etymologically, "the concealed god;"[1] and the idea of Ammon was that of a recondite, incomprehensible divinity, remote from man, hidden, mysterious, the proper object of the profoundest reverence. Practically, this idea was too abstract, too high-flown, too metaphysical, for ordinary minds to conceive of it; and so Ammon was at an early date conjoined with Ra, the

---

[1] Manetho ap. Plutarch, "De Isid. et Osir." s. 9; Iamblich. "De Mysteriis," viii. 3.

Sun, and worshipped as Ammon-Ra,[1] a very intelligible god, neither more nor less than the physical sun, the source of light and life, "the lord of existences and support of all things."[2]

Khem was the generative principle, the power of life and growth in nature. He was rudely and coarsely represented as a mummied figure, with phallus in front, and forms an unsightly object in the sculptures. He presided primarily over the vegetable world, and was the giver of fertility and increase, the lord of the harvest, and the patron of agriculture. But the human species and the various kinds of animals were also under his charge, and from him obtained continuance. He is called, "the king of the gods," "the lifter

AMMON.

of the hand," "the lord of the crown," "the powerful,"[3] and further bears the special title of Kamutf, "bull of his mother," in allusion to the relation which he bore to Nature.

[1] See "Records of the Past," vol. ii. pp. 21, 31, etc.; vol. iv. pp. 11, 16, etc.

[2] *Ibid.* vol. ii. p. 129, l. 12.

[3] "Records of the Past," vol. viii. p. 142.

Kneph was the divine spirit or soul considered as forming the scheme of creation. His name is by some connected etymologically with the Egyptian word for "breath,"[1] which is *nef;* and curious analogies are traced between him and the third Person of the Holy Trinity in the Christian system.[2] As "the Spirit of God" at the time of the creation "moved upon the face of the waters," so Kneph is represented as the deity who presides over the inundations. As the heavens were made by the "breath of God's mouth," so Kneph is called, "the god who has made the sun and moon to revolve under the heaven and above the world, and who has made the world and all that is in it."[3] Some representations exhibit him as a potter with his wheel; and the inscriptions accompanying them assign to him the formation of gods and men. It is perhaps as a procreating principle that he is figured commonly with the head of a ram. Kneph was worshipped chiefly in Upper Egypt, at Elephantine and the Cataracts; but he was acknowledged also at Thebes, at Antæopolis, and elsewhere.

Phthah, whom the Greeks identified with their Hephaistos, and the Romans with their Vulcan, was a creator of a more vulgar type than Kneph or Khem. He was an artisan god, the actual manipulator of matter, and direct maker of the sun, the moon, and the earth. He is called, "the father of the be-

[1] Bunsen, "Egypt's Place," vol. i. p. 375.
[2] Wilkinson, "Ancient Egyptians," vol. iv. p. 236.
[3] Bunsen, vol. i. p. 377.

ginnings," "the first of the gods of the upper world," "he who adjusts the world by his hand," "the lord of the beautiful countenance," and "the

PHTHAH.

lord of truth."[1] He is also defined by an ancient writer [2] as "the god who creates with truth." We find him represented under three quite different forms, as a man walking or sitting, as a mummied figure, accompanied by "the emblem of stability," and as a pigmy or dwarf. A figure of this last description provoked the ridicule of Cambyses,

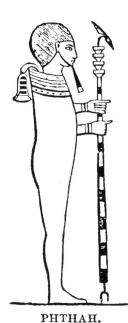

PHTHAH.

the Persian conqueror of Egypt, who "entered the grand temple of Phthah at Memphis, and made great sport of the image."[3] Forms of Phthah are also found consisting of two figures placed back to back, and even of three figures placed at an angle. These seem, however, to represent combinations of Phthah with other nearly allied gods, and are called commonly "figures of Phthah-Sokari," or of "Phthah-Sokari-Osiris."

Ra was the Egyptian sun-god, and was especially

---

[1] "Records of the Past," vol. viii. pp. 5–15; Birch, Guide to the British Museum," p. 13.

[2] Iamblichus, "De Mysteriis," viii. 3.

[3] Herod. iii. 37.

worshipped at Heliopolis. Obelisks, according to some,[1] represented his rays, and were always, or usually, erected in his honour. Heliopolis was cer-

R.A.

tainly one of the places which were thus adorned, for one of the few which still stand erect in Egypt is on the site of that city.[2] The kings for the most part considered Ra their special patron and protector; nay, they went so far as to identify themselves with him, to use his titles as their own, and to adopt his name as the ordinary prefix to their own names and titles. This is believed by many to have been the origin of the word Pharaoh,[3] which was, it is thought, the Hebrew rendering of Ph' Ra = "the sun." Ra is sometimes represented simply by a disk, colored red, or by such a disk with the *ankh*, or symbol of life, attached to it; but more commonly he has the figure of a man, with a hawk's head, and above it the disk, accompanied by plumes, or by a serpent. The beetle (scarabæus) was one of his

[1] Zoega, "De Obeliscis;" Plin. "H. N." xxxvi. 8, s. 14.

[2] See the Frontispiece of this book.

[3] So Wilkinson (in Rawlinson's "Herodotus," vol. ii. p. 181, note 1) and others. But the derivation from *Ph'ouro*, "the king," is perhaps as probable.

emblems.　As for his titles, they are too numerous to mention : the "Litany of Ra"[1] alone contains some hundreds of them.

Osiris was properly a form of Ra.　He was the light of the lower world, the sun from the time that he sinks below the horizon in the west to the hour when he reappears above the eastern horizon in the morning.　This physical idea was, however, at a later date modified, and Osiris was generally recognized as the perpetually presiding lord of the lower world, the king and the judge of Hades or Amenti. His worship was universal throughout Egypt,[2] but his chief temples were at Abydos and Philæ.　Ordinarily he was represented in a mummied form as the god of the dead, but sometimes he appears as a living man, standing or walking.　He carries in his two hands the crook and the flagellum or whip, and commonly wears on his head the crown of Upper Egypt, with a plume of ostrich feather on either side of it. A special character of goodness attaches to him.　We find him called, "the manifester of good," "full of goodness and truth," "the beneficent spirit," "beneficent in will and words," "mild of heart," "and fair and beloved of all who see him."[3]

Neith, or Net, the goddess of Sais, was identified by the Greeks[4] with their Athéne (Minerva), but

---

[1] See " Records of the Past," vol. viii. pp. 105–128.

[2] Herod. ii. 42, with Wilkinson's note.

[3] " Records of the Past," vol. iv. pp. 99–103 ;　Wilkinson, " Ancient Egyptians," vol. iv. p. 320.

[4] Plat. " Tim." p. 22, A ; Cic. " De Nat. Deor." iii. p. 248.

does not appear to have been really a goddess of wisdom. She was the female correspondent of Khem, the conceptive element in nature, as he was the generative. Her titles are, "the mother," "the mistress of heaven," "the elder goddess." [1] She is represented in the form of a woman standing, and wearing on her head the crown of Lower Egypt. In her left hand she carries a sceptre, sometimes accompanied by a bow and two arrows; in her right she bears the *ankh*, or symbol of life. One of the signs with which her name is written resembles a shuttle; from which fact, combined with her carrying a bow and arrows, she has been called, "the goddess of war and weaving." [2] Her worship was not very widely spread, nor is she often mentioned in the inscriptions.

No part of the Egyptian religion was so much developed and so multiplex as their sun worship. [3] Besides Ra and Osiris there were at least six other deities who had a distinctly solar character. These were Shu, Aten, Horus or Harmachis, Tum or Atum, Khepra, and Mentu. Shu was the sun's light, Aten the sun's disk, Har, or Har-em-akhu (Horus or Harmachis), the sun at his rising; Tum (or Atum) the same luminary at his setting; Khepra was the life-giving power of the sun; while Mentu was a provin-

---

[1] Bunsen, "Egypt's Place," vol. i. p. 386; Wilkinson, "Ancient Egyptians," vol. iv. p. 285.

[2] Birch, "Guide to Museum," p. 13.

[3] Birch goes as far as to say, that "most of the gods were connected with the sun, and represented that luminary in its passage through the upper or lower hemisphere" ("Guide," p. 11); but this seems to be an exaggeration.

cial sun-god, adopted into the general pantheon. Athor, moreover, the mother of Ra, and Isis, the sister and wife of Osiris, were in some sort sun-goddesses, and bore upon their heads the disk of Ra, to mark their close connection with the great luminary.

THOTH.

Compared with the worship of the sun, that of the moon was quite secondary and insignificant. Two gods only, Khons and Thoth, had properly speaking, a lunar character.[1] Of these Khons was the moon-god simply, while Thoth combined with his lunar aspect, somewhat curiously, the character of " the god

---

[1] Representations of Osiris are found as Osiris-Aah (Birch, "Guide to Museum," p. 15), or "Osiris, the moon god;" but these are purely abnormal.

2

of letters." He was represented with the head of an ibis; and the ibis and cynocephalous ape were sacred to him. Both he and Khons commonly bear on their heads a crescent and disk, emblematic respectively of the new and the full moon.

Other deities of some importance in the religious system were Maut, the consort of Ammon, who represented matter or nature; Sati, the consort of Kneph, a sort of Egyptian Juno; Sekhet, the consort of Phthah, usually represented as lion-headed, or cat-headed; Seb, the Egyptian Saturn; Hanhar (Onuris), the Egyptian Mars; Sabak or Savak, the crocodile-headed god; Anuke, a war goddess; Nebta (Nephthys), sister of Osiris and Isis; Nut or Netpe, goddess of the firmament; and Ma, goddess of truth. The Egyptians had also gods of taste and touch, of silence, of writing, of medicine, of the harvest, etc. Almost any fact of nature, almost any act of man, might be taken separately and personified, the personification becoming thenceforth a god or goddess.

A class of deities possessing a very peculiar character remains to be noticed. These are the malevolent deities. Set or Sutech, the great enemy of Osiris, a god with the head of a griffin or giraffe; Bes, according to some,[1] the god of death; Taouris the wife of Bes; and Apap, or Apepi, the great serpent, generally represented as slain by Horus.[2] All these

---

[1] So Wilkinson ("Ancient Egyptians," vol. iv. p. 431). Others regard Bes as simply a name of Set or Typhon (Birch, " Dictionary of Hieroglyphics," p. 581).

[2] Wilkinson, "Ancient Egyptians," " Supplement," pl. 42.

were distinctly malignant and evil deities; their representations were, in every case, more or less hideous and grotesque; they were all feared and hated, but nevertheless worshipped; their figures were worn as charms, and even temples were built in their honour.

While the entire pantheon of Egypt was thus multiform and manifold, practically the deities who

TRIAD OF SAVAK-RA, ATHOR, AND KHONS.

received worship in each several town and district were but few.   Local triads were almost universally recognised, and in each place its special triad monopolised, so to say, the religious regards of the inhabitants.[1]   At Memphis, the established triad con-

---

[1] "Egypt from the Earliest Times," "Introduction," p. xi.; Wilkinson, "Ancient Egyptians," vol. iv. pp. 230–233.

sisted of Phthah, Sekhet, and Tum; at Thebes, of
Ammon-Ra, Maut, and Khons; at Heliopolis of Ra,
Nebhept (= Athor), and Horus; at Elephantine of
Kneph, Sati, and Anuke; at Abydos, of Osiris, Isis,
and Horus; at Ombos, of Savak, Athor, and Khons;
at Silsilis, of Ra, Phthah, and the Nile god, Hapi or
Neilus.   Sometimes a fourth god or goddess was
associated with the principal three, as Bast at Memphis, Neith at Thebes, Nephthys at Abydos, and
Hak at Elephantine; but the fourth was always
quite subordinate.   Occasionally a city recognized
more than one triad; for instance, Silsilis held in
honour, besides Ra, Phthah, and Hapi, a triad consisting of Set, Thoth, and Netpe; and another comprising Ammon, Ra, and Savak.

Another peculiar feature of the Egyptian religion, and one which, though it may have had some
redeeming points,[1] must be pronounced on the whole
low and degrading, was the worship of live animals.
In the first instance, certain animals seem to have
been assumed as emblems of certain gods,[2] from some
real or fancied analogy; after which, in course of
time, the animals themselves came to be regarded
as sacred; specimens of them were attached to the
temples, kept in shrines, and carefully fed and nur-

---

[1] The sacred character of cows and heifers secured a continual
increase in the stock of cattle; that of cats and ichneumons, of
ibises, hawks, and vultures, preserved those useful animals, of
which the two former kept the houses free from mice and snakes,
while the three latter were admirable scavengers.

[2] As the vulture of Maut, the ibis of Thoth, and the ram of
Kneph, etc.

tured during life, and at death embalmed and buried in sacred repositories, while the entire species had a sacred character assigned to it universally or partially. Animals of these kinds it was unlawful to kill, either in Egypt generally, or within the limits within which they were honoured; if they died, their death was mourned, and they were carefully buried by those who found them, or to whom they belonged, with more or less ceremony.[1] Of animals universally sacred the principal were cows and heifers, which were sacred to Athor; cynocephalous apes and ibises, which were sacred to Thoth; cats, which were sacred to Bast; hawks, which were sacred to Ra; and perhaps asps, though this is uncertain.[2] Sheep, especially rams, were generally regarded as sacred, being emblems of Kneph; and dogs, though not assigned to any special deity, held a similar position.

The worship of other animals had a more local character. Lions, emblems of Horus and Tum, were sacred at Leontopolis; crocodiles, emblems of Savak, at Crocodilopolis and in the Fayoum generally; wolves or jackals, emblems of Anubis, at Lycopolis; shrew-mice, emblems of Maut, at Buto and Athribis; hippopotami, emblems of Set and Taouris, at Papremis; antelopes at Coptos; ibexes and frogs at Thebes; goats at Mendu; vultures at Eileithyia; fish at Latopolis; ichneumons at Heracleopolis; and other animals elsewhere. Each town was jealous for the honour of its special

[1] Herod. ii. 66, 67, with Wilkinson's notes.
[2] So Wilkinson, "Ancient Egyptians," vol. v. p. 243.

favourites; and quarrels broke out between city and city, or between province and province, in connection with their sacred animals, which led in some cases to violent and prolonged conflicts, in others to a smouldering but permanent hostility. It is difficult to say how much of the religious sentiment of the nation was absorbed by these unworthy objects; but there is no just ground for believing that the animal worship, absurd as it may have been, interfered seriously with the reverence and respect which were paid to the proper deities.

The worst, and most pronounced form of the animal worship has still to be mentioned. In some instances the belief was, not that a particular class of animals had a sacred character, but that a deity absolutely became incarnate in an individual animal, and so remained till its death. Animals to which this was supposed to have happened were actual gods, and received the most profound veneration that it was possible to pay. Such were the Apis bulls, of which a succession was maintained at Memphis, in the temple of Phthah, incarnations, according to some, of Phthah,[1] according to others of Osiris,[2] which were among the objects of worship most venerated by the Egyptians. Such, again, were the Mnevis bulls of Heliopolis, incarnations of Ra or Tum, and the Bacis or Pacis bulls of Hermonthis, incarnations of Horus. These beasts, maintained at the cost of the

[1] See Birch, " Egypt from the Earliest Times," " Introduction," p. xii.

[2] Wilkinson, in Rawlinson's " Herodotus," vol. ii. p. 428, note 2.

priestly communities in the great temples of their respective cities, were perpetually adored and prayed
to by thousands during their lives, and at their deaths
were entombed with the utmost care in huge sarcophagi, while all Egypt went into mourning on account of their decease.

The external manifestation of religion in Egypt
was magnificent and splendid. Nowhere did religious
ceremonial occupy a larger part in the life of a people.
In each city and town, one or more grand structures
upreared themselves above the rest of the buildings,
enriched with all that Egyptian art could supply of
painted and sculptured decoration, dedicated to the
honour and bearing the name of some divinity or
divinities. The image of the great god of the place
occupied the central shrine, accompanied in most instances by two or three contemplar gods or goddesses.
Around were the chambers of the priests, and further
off court after court, some pillared, some colonnaded
and all more or less adorned with sculpture and paint-
ing, the entrance to them lying through long avenues
of sphinxes or obelisks, which conducted to the
propylæa, two gigantic towers flanking the main
doorway.[1] A perpetual ceremonial of the richest kind
went on within the temple walls ; scores of priests,
with shaven heads and clean white linen garments,[2]
crowded the courts and corridors ; long proces-

---

[1] These towers have been compared, with some reason, to those
which commonly adorn the western façade of our cathedrals.
(Fergusson, " History of Architecture," vol. i. p. 117.)

[2] Herod. ii. 37.

sions made their way up or down the sphinx avenues, incense floated in the air, strains of music resounded without pause, hundreds of victims were sacrificed ; everywhere a holiday crowd, in bright array, cheerful and happy, bore its part in the festival, and made the courts re-echo with their joyous acclamations. The worship was conducted chiefly by means of rhythmic litanies or hymns, in which prayer and praise were blended, the latter predominating.[1] Ceremony followed ceremony. The calendar was crowded with festivals : and a week rarely passed without the performance of some special rite, some annual observance, having its own peculiar attractions. Foreigners beheld with astonishment the almost perpetual round of religious services, which engaged, or at any rate seemed to engage, the main attention of all ranks of the people.

Belief in a future life was a main principle of the Egyptian religion. Immediately after death, the soul, it was taught, descended into the lower world (Amenti), and was conducted to the "Hall of Truth," where it was judged in the presence of Osiris, and of his forty-two assessors, the "Lords of Truth," and judges of the dead. Anubis, the son of Osiris, who was called "the director of the weight," brought forth a pair of scales, and after placing in one scale a figure or emblem of Truth, set in the other a vase

---

[1] See the "Litany of Ra," and the "Hymns" to Osiris, Amen, Amen-Ra., and Ra-Harmachis, published in "Records of the Past," vol. ii. pp. 105–134; vol. iv. pp. 99–104; vol. vi. pp. 99–101; and vol. viii. pp. 131–134.

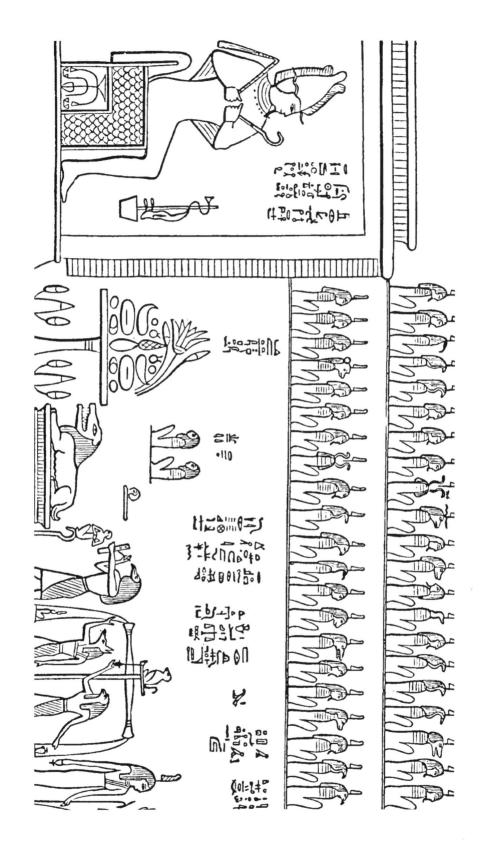

containing the good deeds of the deceased, Thoth
standing by the while, with a tablet in his hand,
whereon to record the result.[1] If the good deeds
were sufficient, if they weighed down the scale wherein they were placed, then the happy soul was permitted to enter "the boat of the sun," and was conducted by good spirits to the Elysian fields (Aahlu),
to the " Pools of Peace," and the dwelling-places of
the blest. If, on the contrary, the good deeds were
insufficient, if the scale remained suspended in the
air, then the unhappy soul was sentenced, according
to the degree of its ill deserts, to go through a round
of transmigrations in the bodies of animals more or
less unclean ; the number, nature, and duration of
the transmigrations depending on the degree of the
deceased's demerits, and the consequent length and
severity of the punishment which he deserved, or the
purification which he needed. Ultimately, if after
many trials sufficient purity was not attained, the
wicked soul, which had proved itself incurable,
underwent a final sentence at the hands of Osiris,
judge of the dead, and, being condemned to complete
and absolute annihilation, was destroyed upon the
steps of Heaven by Shu, the Lord of Light.[2] The
good soul, having first been freed from its infirmities
by passing through the basin of purgatorial fire

[1] Wilkinson, "Ancient Egyptians," vol. v. pp. 314, 315. Representations of the scene are frequent in the tombs, and in the
many copies of the "Ritual of the Dead." (See the accompanying wood-cut.)

[2] Birch, "Guide to Museum," pp. 14, 15.

guarded by the four ape-faced genii, was made the
companion of Osiris, for a period of three thousand
years, after which it returned from Amenti, re-en-
tered its former body, rose from the dead, and lived
once more a human life upon the earth. This process
was gone through again and again, until a certain
mystic cycle of years became complete, when, to

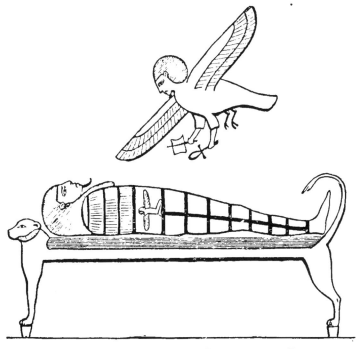

MUMMY AND DISEMBODIED SPIRIT.

crown all, the good and blessed attained the final joy
of union with God, being absorbed into the divine
essence from which they had once emanated, and so
attaining the full perfection and true end of their existence.

With their belief in a future life, and their
opinions regarding the fate of good and bad souls,

were bound up in the closest way their arrangements
with respect to dead bodies, and their careful and
elaborate preparation of tombs.   As each man hoped
to be among those who would be received into Aahlu,
and after dwelling with Osiris for three thousand
years would return to earth, and re-enter their old
bodies, it was requisite that bodies should be enabled
to resist decay for that long period.   Hence the entire system of embalming, of swathing in linen, and
then burying in stone sarcophagi covered with lids
that it was scarcely possible to lift, or even to move.
Hence if a man was wealthy, he spent enormous sums
on making himself a safe and commodious, an elegant
and decorated tomb; either piling a pyramid over
his sarcophagus, or excavating deep into the solid
rock, and preparing for his resting-place a remote
chamber at the end of a long series of galleries.
With the notion, probably, that it would be of use to
him in his passage through Amenti to Aahlu, he
took care to have the most important passages from
the sacred book entitled the " Ritual of the Dead,"
either inscribed on the inner part of the coffin in
which he was to lie, or painted on his mummy ban-
dages, or engraved upon the inner walls of his tomb.[1]
Sometimes he even had a complete copy of the book
buried with him, no doubt for reference, if his memory failed to supply him with the right invocation or
prayer at the dangerous parts of his long journey.

The thought of death, of judgment, of a sentence
to happiness or misery according to the life led on

<hr />

[1] Bunsen, "Egypt's Place," vol. v. pp. 127–129.

earth, was thus familiar to the ordinary Egyptian. His theological notions were confused and fantastical; but he had a strong and abiding conviction that his fate after death would depend on his conduct during his life on earth, and especially on his observance of the moral law and performance of his various duties.[1]

The better educated Egyptian had a firmer grasp of the truths of natural religion. Below the popular mythology there lay concealed from general view, but open to the educated classes, a theological system which was not far removed from pure "natural theology." The real essential unity of the divine nature was taught and insisted on. The sacred texts spoke of a single being, "the sole producer of all things in heaven and earth, himself not produced of any," "the only true living God, self-originated," "who exists from the beginning," "who has made all things, but has not himself been made."[2] This

[1] See Birch, "Egypt from the Earliest Times," p. 46:—"The Egyptian enjoyed all the pleasures of existence, and delighted more in the arts of peace than war. In his religious belief the idea of a future state, and probably of the transmigration of souls, was ever present to his mind, while—and his long life was one preparation for death—to be devoted or pious to the gods, obedient to the wishes of his sovereign, affectionate towards his wife and children, were the maxims inculcated for his domestic or inner life. Beyond that circle his duties to mankind were comprised in giving bread to the hungry, drink to the thirsty, clothes to the naked, oil to the wounded, and burial to the dead. On the exercise of good works he rested his hopes of passing the ordeal of the future and great judgment, and reaching the Aahlu or Elysian fields, and Pools of Peace of the Egyptian paradise."

[2] Lenormant, "Manuel d'Histoire Ancienne," vol. i. p. 522.

being seems never to have been represented by any material, even symbolical form.[1] It is thought that he had no name, or, if he had, that it must have been unlawful to pronounce or write it.[2] Even Ammon, the "concealed God," was a mere external adumbration of this mysterious and unapproachable deity. He was a pure spirit, perfect in every respect, all-wise, all-mighty, supremely, perfectly good.

Those who grasped this great truth understood clearly that the many gods of the popular mythology were mere names, personified attributes of the one true Deity, or parts of the nature which he had created, considered as informed and inspired by him. Num or Kneph represented the creative mind, Phthah the creative hand, or act of creating; Maut represented matter, Ra the sun, Khons the moon, Seb the earth, Khem the generative power in nature, Keith the conceptive power, Nut the upper hemisphere of heaven, Athor the lower world or under hemisphere; Thoth personified the divine wisdom, Ammon the divine mysteriousness or incomprehensibility, Osiris the divine goodness. It may not be always easy to say what is the exact quality, act, or part of nature which is represented by each god and goddess; but the principle was clear and beyond a doubt. No educated Egyptian priest certainly, pro-

Similar phrases are frequent in all the religious inscriptions. (See "Records of the Past," vol. ii. pp. 129–132; vol. iv. pp. 99 100; vol. vi. 100, etc.)

[1] Wilkinson, "Ancient Egyptians, vol. iv. p. 178."

bably no educated layman, conceived of the popular gods as really separate and distinct beings. All knew that there was but one god, and understood that when worship was offered to Khem, or Phthah, or Maut, or Thoth, or Ammon, the one god was worshipped under some one of his forms, or in some one of his aspects. Hence, in the solemn hymns and chants, which were composed by the priests to be used in the various festivals, the god who is for the time addressed receives all the highest titles of honour, and even has the names of other gods freely assigned to him, as being in some sort identical with them. Thus in one hymn, Hapi, the Nile god, is invoked as Ammon and Phthah;[1] in another, Osiris as Ra and Thoth;[2] while in a third Ra is Khem and Ammon, Tum and Horus and Khepra all in one,[3] and though spoken of as "begotten of Phthah,"[4] is "the good god," "the chief of all the gods," "the ancient of heaven," "the lord of all existences," "the support of all things."[5]

It is not altogether easy to say what the educated Egyptian believed with respect to evil. The myth of Osiris represented him as persecuted by his brother, Set or Sutech, who murdered him and cut up his body into several pieces, after which he was made war upon by Horus, Osiris' son, and in course of

---

[1] "Records of the Past," vol. iv. p. 107, ll. 4 and 11.

[2] *Ibid.* p.103, par. 24, *ad fin.*

[3] *Ibid.* vol. ii. pp. 130, 131, and 133.

[4] *Ibid.* p. 129, l. 20.

[5] *Ibid.* ll. 2–12.

time deposed and thrust down to darkness.[1]   In the latter mythology Set and Bes, Taouris and Apepi were distinctly malignant beings, personifications, apparently, of an evil principle; and from the inscriptions and papyri of this period, we should gather that the Egyptian religion was dualistic, and comprised the idea of a constant and interminable struggle between the powers of light and darkness, of good and evil; a struggle in which there was some superiority on the part of good, but no complete victory, not even a very decided preponderance.   On the other hand, as we go back and examine carefully the more ancient monuments and the earlier writings, we find less and less trace of this antagonism; we find Set or Sutech spoken of as "great," "glorious;"[2] we find that the kings identify themselves with him,[3] build him magnificent temples, and make him numerous offerings.[4]   It is doubtful whether at this time any notion existed of evil or malignancy attaching to Set.   If it did, we must suppose the early creed to have been that "the bad was a necessary part of the universal system, and inherent in all things equally with the good;"[5] and so, that divine honours were due to the gods representing the principles of disorder and evil no less than to those representing the opposite principles.   The change of view with

---

[1] Wilkinson, "Ancient Egyptians," vol. iv. pp. 329–333.

[2] "Records of the Past," vol. iv. p. 29.

[3] *Ibid.* vol. ii. p. 76 ; vol. viii. p. 75.

[4] *Ibid.* vol. iv. p. 27 ; vol. viii. pp. 27–31.

[5] So Wilkinson, "Ancient Egyptians," vol. iv. p. 423.

regard to Set may have been connected to some extent with national rivalries, for Set was, beyond a doubt, the special god of the Hyksos,[1] the foreign conquerors of Egypt, whom after-ages detested, and also of the Khita or Hittites,[2] with whom the Pharaohs of the eighteenth, nineteenth, and twentieth dynasties were engaged in constant hostilities.

It has been maintained by some that the religion of the educated Egyptians comprised a recognition of the doctrine of the Trinity. The learned Cudworth in the seventeenth century undertook to prove that a doctrine closely resembling the Christian had been taught by the Egyptian priests many centuries before Christ,[3] and some moderns have caught at his statements, and laid it down that the doctrine of the Trinity may be traced to an Egyptian source. But there is really not the slightest ground for this assertion. Cudworth's arguments were long ago met and refuted by Mosheim;[4] and modern investigation of the Egyptian remains has but confirmed Mosheim's conclusions. The Egyptians held the unity of God; but their unity had within it no trinity. God with them was absolutely one in essence, and when divided up, was divided, not into three, but into a multitude of aspects. It is true that they had a fancy for triads; but a triad is not a Trinity. The triads

[1] Birch, "Egypt from the Earliest Times," p. 75; "Records of the Past," vol. viii. p. 3.

[2] "Records of the Past," vol. iv. pp. 31, 32.

[3] See the "Intellectual System of the Universe," ch. v. p. 413.

[4] In the Latin translation of Cudworth's great work, notes to p. 413.

3

are not groups of persons, but of attributes; the
three are not cocqual, but distinctly the reverse, the
third in the triad being always subordinate; nor is
the division regarded as in any case exhaustive of
the divine nature, or exclusive of other divisions.
Moreover, as already observed, the triad is frequently
enlarged by the addition of a fourth person or character, who is associated as closely with the other
three as they are with each other. Cudworth's
view must therefore be set aside as altogether imagi-
nary; and the encomiast of the Egyptian religion
must content himself with pointing out that a real
monotheism underlay the superficial polytheism, without requiring us to believe that even the wisest of
the priests had any knowledge of the greatest of all
Christian mysteries.[1]

[1] See Latin translation of Cudworth's great work, p. 28.

CHAPTER II.

THE RELIGION OF THE ASSYRIANS AND BABYLONIANS.

"Bel boweth down, Nebo stoopeth."—ISAIAH xlvi. 1.
"Merodach is broken in pieces."—JER. l. 2.

THE Babylonian and Assyrian polytheism differed from the Egyptian, in the first place, by being less multitudinous,[1] and in the second, by having, far more than the Egyptian, an astral character. The Mesopotamian system was, moreover, so far as appears, what the Egyptian was not, a belief in really distinct gods. The great personages of the pantheon have for the most part their own peculiar offices and attributes; they do not pass the one into the other; they do not assume each other's names; they do not combine so as to produce a single deity out of several. We have no indication in the literary remains of Babylon or Assyria of any esoteric religion, no evidence on which we can lay it down that the conceptions of the educated upon religious subjects differed seriously from those of the lowest

[1] It is true that the inscriptions speak in a vague way of "four thousand," and even of the "five thousand gods" ("Records of the Past," vol. vii. p. 128; Rawlinson, "Ancient Monarchies," vol. i. p. 155, note 9). But, practically, there are not more than about twenty deities who obtain frequent mention.

35

ranks of worshippers.[1] Berosus, who was a Chaldæan priest, and who should, therefore, if there was any such system, have been well acquainted with it, has in his extant fragments nothing monotheistic, nothing to distinguish his religious views from those of the mass of his countrymen. According to all appearance, the religion of the Babylonians and Assyrians was thus a real polytheism, a worship of numerous divinities, whom it was not thought necessary to trace to a single stock,[2] who were essentially on a par the one with the other, and who divided among them the religious regards of the people.

An account of the Assyrian and Babylonian religion must thus be, in the main, an account of their pantheon. From the character of their gods, from the actions and attributes assigned to them, from the material representations under which they showed them forth, we must gather the tone of their religious thought, the nature of the opinions which they entertained concerning the mysterious powers above them and beyond them, whom they recognized as divine beings.

In each country, at the head of the pantheon stood a god, not the origin of the others, nor in any real sense the fountain of divinity, but of higher rank and dignity than the rest, *primus inter pares*, ordina-

---

[1] The late Mr. Fox Talbot expressed in 1873 a somewhat different opinion. (See the "Transactions of the Society of Biblical Archæology," vol. ii. p. 35.) But it does not appear to me that he made out his case.

[2] See the Author's "Ancient Monarchies," vol. i. p. 142.

rily named first, and assigned the titles of greatest honour, and forming the principal or at least the highest object of worship both to the kings and people. This deity is, in Assyria, Asshur; in Babylonia, Il or Ra. Some critics[1] are of opinion that the two gods are essentially one, that the Assyrian Asshur is neither more nor less than Il or Ra localized and regarded as the special god of Assyria, the protector of the Assyrian territory and the tutelary divinity of the Assyrian kings. But this view is not generally accepted, and seems to rest upon no sure foundation. There is a marked difference of character and position between the Babylonian Il and the Assyrian Asshur. Il in the Babylonian system is dim and shadowy; his attributes are, comparatively speaking, indistinct; and his very name is not of frequent occurrence.[2] Asshur in the Assyrian system is, of all the gods, by far the most pronounced and prominent figure. No name occurs so often as his; no god has attributes so clearly marked and positive. On these grounds it has been generally held, that the two are not to be identified, but to be kept distinct, and to be regarded as respectively peculiar to the two nations. We proceed, therefore, to speak of them separately.

Il (or Ra) was, as already remarked, a somewhat

[1] As M. Lenormant. (See his " Manuel d'Histoire Ancienne," vol. ii., p. 182.)

[2] In the six Assyrian volumes of " Records of the Past," I find the name of Il (or El) only four times (vol. v., pp. 21, 129 ; vol. vii., pp. 95, 96). In two of these places it seems to stand for Bel, who is called Bel-El sometimes (*Ibid.* vol. xi., p. 24).

shadowy being. There is a vagueness about the name itself, which means simply " god," and can scarcely be said to connote any particular attribute. The Babylonians never represent his form, and they frequently omit him from lists which seem to contain all the other principal gods.[1] Yet he was certainly regarded as the head of the pantheon, and in the most ancient times must have been acknowledged as the tutelary deity of Babylon itself, which received its name of Bab-il (in Accadian, *Ka-ra*), meaning " the Gate of Il," from him. He seems to have had no special temple, being probably worshipped in all temples by the few persons who were his votaries. His name was, occasionally, but not very frequently, used as an element in the personal appellations of Babylonians.[2]

Asshur, the Assyrian substitute for Il or Ra, was primarily and especially the tutelary deity of Assyria and of the Assyrian monarchs. The land of Assyria bears his name without any modification ; its inhabitants are " his servants " or " his people ; " its troops " the armies of the god Asshur ; " its enemies " the enemies of Asshur." As for the kings, they stand connected with him in respect of almost everything which they do. He places them upon the throne, firmly establishes them in the government, lengthens

[1] As, for instance, that of Agu-kak-rimi in the inscription published in vol. vii. of the " Records," pp. 7, 8, where ten "great gods" are enumerated, viz.: Anu and Anunit, Bel and Beltis, Hea and Davkina, Zira (Zir-banit?), Sin, Shamas, and Merodach, but no mention is made of Il.

[2] " Records of the Past," vol. iii. p. 15 ; vol. ix. p. 99 ; etc.

the years of their reigns, preserves their power, protects their forts and armies, directs their expeditions, gives them victory on the day of battle, makes their name celebrated, multiplies their offspring greatly, and the like. To him they look for the fulfilment of all their wishes, and especially for the establishment of their sons, and their sons' sons, on the Assyrian throne to the remotest ages. Their usual phrase when speaking of him is, "Asshur, my lord." They represent themselves as passing their lives in his service. It is to spread his worship that they carry on their wars. They fight, ravage, destroy in his name. Finally, when they subdue a country, they are careful to "set up the emblems of Asshur," and to make the conquered people conform to his laws.[1]

The ordinary titles of Asshur are, "the great lord," "the king of all the gods," "he who rules supreme over the gods." He is also called, occasionally, "the father of the gods," although that is a title which belongs more properly to Bel. He is figured as a man with a horned cap, and often carrying a bow, issuing from the middle of a winged circle, and either shooting an arrow, or stretching forth his hand, as if to aid or smite. The winged circle by itself is also used as his emblem, and probably denotes his ubiquity and eternity, as the human form does his intelligence, and the horned cap his power. This emblem, with or without the human figure, is an almost invariable accompaniment of Assyrian royalty. The great king

---

[1] "Records of the Past," vol. i. p. 17; vol. iii. pp. 86, 93, 95, 96; vol. v. pp. 14, 15, etc.; vol. ix. pp. 5, 8, 9, etc.

wears it embroidered upon his robes, carries it engraved upon his seal or cylinder, represents it above his head in the rock-tablets whereon he carves his

ASSHUR.

image, stands or kneels in adoration before it, fights under its shadow, under its protection returns victorious, places it conspicuously upon his obelisks. And in all these representations, it is remarkable how he makes the emblem conform to the circumstances in which he is himself engaged at the time. Where he is fighting, Asshur, too, has his arrow upon the string, and points it against the monarch's adversaries. When he is returning home victorious, with the disused bow in his left hand, and his right hand outstretched and elevated, Asshur, too, has the same attitude. In peaceful scenes the bow disappears altogether. If the king worships, the god holds out his hand to aid; if he is engaged in secular acts, the Divine presence is thought to be sufficiently marked by the circle and the wings without the human figure.[1]

In immediate succession to Asshur in Assyria and Il in Babylonia, we find in both countries a triad, consisting of Anu, Bel, and Hea or Hoa. These three are called, *par excellence*, "the great gods."[2] In execrations they are separated off from all the other deities, and placed together in a clause which

[1] See the Author's "Ancient Monarchies," vol. ii. pp. 234, 235.
[2] "Records of the Past," vol. vii. p. 121; vol. ix. pp. 100, 106, etc.

stands at the head of the list of curses. In invocations their names follow, for the most part, immediately after the name of Asshur; and this is their usual and proper position in all complete lists of the chief gods.[1] Anu and Bel in the Babylonian system are brothers, both being sons of Il or Ra; but this relationship is scarcely acknowledged in Assyria. Hoa in both countries stands apart, unconnected with the other two, and, indeed, unconnected with any of the other gods, except with such as are his offspring.

It has been conjectured[2] that in this triad we have a cosmogonic myth, and that the three deities represent, Anu, the primordial chaos, or matter without form; Hoa, life and intelligence, considered as moving in and animating matter; and Bel, the organising and creating spirit, by which matter was actually brought into subjection, and the material universe arranged in an orderly way. But it may be questioned whether the veil which hides the esoteric meaning of the Assyrian religion has been as yet sufficiently lifted to entitle such conjectures to much attention. Our own belief is that Anu, Bel, and Hoa, were originally the gods of the earth, of the heaven, and of the waters, thus corresponding in the main to the classical Pluto, Zeus or Jupiter, and Poseidon or Neptune, who divided between them the

[1] "Records of the Past," vol. iii. p. 83; vol. v. p. 29; vol. vii. p. 7; vol. ix. p. 23, etc.

[2] See Lenormant, "Manuel d'Histoire Ancienne," vol. ii. pp. 182, 183.

dominion over the visible creation. But such notions
became, in course of time, overlaid to a great extent
with others; and though Hoa continued always more
or less of a water deity, Anu and Bel ceased to have
peculiar spheres, and became merely "great gods,"
with a general superintendence over the world, and
with no very marked difference of powers.

Anu is commonly spoken of as "the old Anu,"
"the original chief," "the king of the lower world,"
and "the lord of spirits and demons." There is one
text in which he seems to be called "the father of
the gods," but the reading is doubtful. We cannot
identify as his any of the divine forms on the Assyrian or Babylonian monuments, nor can we assign
to him any emblem, excepting that of the single up-
right wedge, which represents him on the Chaldæan
numeration tablets. This single wedge has the
numerical power of sixty, and sixty appears to have
been assigned to Anu as his special number. Though
a "great god," he was not one towards whom much
preference was shown. His name is scarcely ever
found as an element in royal or other appellations;
the kings do not very often mention him; and only
one monarch speaks of himself as his special votary.[1]

The god Bel, familiarly known to us both from
Scripture[2] and from the Apocrypha,[3] is one of the
most marked and striking figures in the pantheon

[1] Tiglath Pileser I. (see "Records of the Past," vol. v. p. 24.)
Yet even he is still more devoted to Asshur.

[2] Isaiah xlvi. 1; Jer. l. 2; li. 44.

[3] See the history of "Bel and the Dragon."

alike of Babylonia and of Assyria. Bel is "the god of lords," "the father of the gods," "the creator," "the mighty prince," and "the just prince of the gods." He plays a leading part in the mythological legends, which form so curious a feature in the Babylonian and Assyrian religion. In the "History of Creation" we are told that Bel made the earth and the heaven; that he formed man by means of a mixture of his own blood with earth, and also formed beasts; and that afterwards he created the sun and the moon, the stars, and the five planets.[1] In the "War of the Gods," we find him contending with the great dragon, Tiamat, and after a terrible single combat destroying her by flinging a thunderbolt into her open mouth.[2] He also, in conjunction with Hoa, plans the defence when the seven spirits of evil rise in rebellion, and the dwelling-place of the gods is assaulted by them.[3] The titles of Bel generally express dominion. He is "the lord," *par excellence*, which is the exact meaning of his name in Assyrian; he is "the king of all the spirits," "the lord of the world," and again, "the lord of all the countries." Babylon and Nineveh are, both of them, under his special care; Nineveh having the title of "the city of Bel," in some passages of the inscriptions. The chief seat of the worship of Bel in Babylonia was Nipur, now Niffer, and in Assyria, Calah, now Nimrud. He had also a temple at Duraba (Akkerkuf).

---

[1] Berosus ap. Euseb. "Chron. Can." i. 3.

[2] "Records of the Past," vol. ix. pp. 137–139.

[3] *Ibid.* vol. v. p. 164.

Hea or Hoa, the third god of the first triad, ranks immediately after Bel in the complete lists of Assyrian deities. He is emphatically one of the "great gods," and is called, "the king," "the great inventor," and "the determiner of destinies." We have already remarked that he was specially connected with the element of water; and hence he is "the king of the deep," "the king of rivers," "the lord of fountains," and, to a certain extent, "the lord of the harvest." In the legend of creation he is joined with Bel, in the office of guardian, and watches over the regularity of the planetary courses.[1] In the "War of the Gods," he and Bel plan the defence, after which Hea commits the executions of the plans made to his son, Marduk or Merodach.[2] In the flood legend, Hea naturally plays an important part. It is he who announces to Hasis-adra, the Babylonian Noah, that a deluge is about to destroy mankind, and commands him to build a great ship, in order that he may escape it.[3] It is he again who opposes the wish of Bel to make the destruction complete, and persuades him to let Hasis-adra and his family come out safe from the ark.[4] In the tale of Ishtar's descent into Hades, Hea's counsel is sought by the moon-god; and by a skilful device he obtains the restoration of the Queen of Love to the upper world.[5] Indeed, throughout the whole of the mythology we find all clever inventions and well-laid

[1] "Records of the Past," vol. ix. p. 118.
[2] *Ibid.* vol. v. p. 165.   [3] *Ibid.* vol. vii. pp. 135, 136.
[4] *Ibid.* p. 142.   [5] *Ibid.* vol. i. pp. 147–149.

plans ascribed to him, so that his history quite justifies his title of "lord of deep thoughts." Hea is probably intended by the Oe of Helladius,[1] and the Oannes of Berosus,[2] who came up out of the Persian Gulf, and instructed the first settlers on the Lower Tigris and Euphrates in letters, science, religion, law, and agriculture.

In direct succession to the three gods of the first triad, Anu, Bel, and Hea or Hoa, we find a second still more widely recognised triad, comprising the moon-god, the sun-god, and the god of the atmosphere. There is great difference of opinion with respect to the name of the last god of these three, which is never spelt phonetically in the inscriptions, but only represented by a monogram. He has been called Iva (or Yav), Vul, Bin, Yem (or Im), and recently Rimmon.[3] Without presuming to decide this vexed question, we propose to adopt provisionally the rendering "Vul," as the one likely to be most familiar to our readers, from its employment by Sir Henry Rawlinson, Mr. George Smith, and Mr. Fox Talbot. We shall speak therefore of the second triad as one consisting of Sin, Shamas, and Vul, the gods respectively of the moon, the sun, and the atmosphere.

It is very noticeable that in Assyria and Babylonia the moon-god took precedence of the sun-god.

---

[1] Ap. Phot. "Bibliothec" cclxxxix. p. 1594.

[2] Berosus ap. Euseb. "Chron. Can." l. s. c.

[3] "Transactions of the Society of Biblical Archæology," vol. v. p. 441; "Records of the Past," vol. v. p. 29; vol. vii. pp. 165, 170; vol. ix. pp. 23, 27, etc.

Night probably was more agreeable to the inhabitants of those hot regions than day; and the cool,
placid time when they could freely contemplate the
heavens, and make their stellar and other obser-
vations, was especially grateful to the priestly astronomers who had the superintendence and arrangement of the religion. Sin, the moon, is thus one of
the leading deities. He is called, "the chief of the
gods of heaven and earth," "the king of the gods,"
and even "the god of the gods."[1] These seem,
however, to be hyperbolical expressions, used by his
votaries in the warmth of their hearts, when in the
stage of religion which Professor Max Muller has
designated "Henotheism."[2] Sin more properly was
"the brilliant," "the illuminator," "he who dwells
in the sacred heavens," "he who circles round the
heavens," and "the lord of the month." Again, for
some recondite reason, which is not explained, he was
selected to preside over architecture, and in this connection he is "the supporting architect," "the
strengthener of fortifications," and, more generally,
"the lord of building."

A close bond of sympathy united Sin with the
two other members of the second triad. When the
seven spirits of evil made war in heaven, and directed their main attack upon Sin, as the chief leader of
the angelic host, Shamas and Vul instantly came to
his aid, withstood the spirits, and, fighting firmly

[1] In the Inscription of Nabonidus. (See "Records of the Past,"
vol. v. pp. 146, 147.)

[2] "Contemporary Review," Nov. 1878, pp. 722.

side by side with him, succeeded in repulsing them.[1] The three are frequently conjoined in invocations, execrations, and the like.[2] In offerings and festivals, however, Sin is united with Shamas only, the place of Vul being taken by a goddess who is entitled " the divine mistress of the world."[3]

Sin was among the gods most widely and devoutly worshipped, both in Babylonia and Assyria. He had temples at Ur, Babylon, Borsippa, Calah, and Dur-Sargina. The third month of the year, called Sivan, was dedicated to him. In a month not so dedicated we find sacrifice to the moon prescribed on nine days out of the thirty.[4] His name was widely used as an element in royal and other appellations, as, for instance, in the well-known name, Sennacherib, which in the original is *Sin-akhi-irib*, or " Sin has multiplied brothers."

SIN.

Shamas, the sun-god, occupies the middle position in the second triad, which is either " Sin, Shamas, Vul," or " Vul, Shamas, Sin," though more commonly the former. His titles are either general or special. In a general way he is called, " the establisher of heaven and earth," " the judge of heaven

---

[1] See " Records of the Past," vol. v. pp. 164–166.

[2] *Ibid.* vol. i. pp. 57, 93, etc.; vol. v. pp. 7, 122, 123; vol. ix. pp. 23, 100, etc.

[3] "Records of the Past," vol. vii. pp. 159, 162, etc.

[4] See the calendar referred to in the last note, where sacrifices to Sin are prescribed for the 1st, 2nd, 13th, 14th, 18th, 20th, 21st, 22nd, and 29th days of the month.

and earth," "the warrior of the world," and "the regent of all things," while, with direct reference to his physical nature, he is "the lord of fire," "the light of the gods," "the ruler of the day," and "he who illumines the expanse of heaven and earth."

The kings regard him as affording them especial help in war. He is "the supreme ruler, who casts a favorable eye on expeditions," the "vanquisher of the king's enemies," "the breaker-up of opposition." He "casts his motive influence" over the monarchs, and causes them to "assemble their chariots and their warriors," he "goes forth with their armies," and enables them to extend their dominions; he chases their enemies before them, causes opposition to cease, and brings them back with victory to their own country.

Besides this, in time of peace, he helps them to sway the sceptre of power, and to rule over their subjects with authority. It seems that, from observing the manifest agency of the material sun in stimulating all the functions of nature, the Assyrians and Babylonians came to the conclusion that the sun-god exerted a similar influence over the minds of men, and was the great motive agent in human history.[1]

The worship of Shamas was universal. The seventh month, Tisri, was dedicated to him, and in the second Elul, he had, like the moon-god, nine festivals. His emblem appears upon almost all the religious cylinders, and in almost all lists of the gods his name holds a high place. Sometimes he is a

[1] "Ancient Monarchies," vol. i. p. 160.

member of a leading triad, composed of himself together with Sin and Asshur.[1] In the mythological legends he is not very frequently mentioned. We find him, however, defending the moon-god, in conjunction with Vul, when the seven spirits make their assault upon heaven ;[2] and in the deluge tablets we are told that it was he who actually made the Flood.[3] But otherwise the mythology is silent about him, offering in this respect a remarkable contrast to the Egyptian, where the sun is the principal figure.

Vul, the god of the atmosphere, who completes the second triad, has, on the whole, a position quite equal to that of Sin and Shamas, whom he occasionally even precedes in the lists.[4] Some kings seem to place him on a par with Anu, or with Asshur, recognising Anu and Vul, or Asshur and Vul, as especially "the great gods," and as their own peculiar guardians.[5] In a general way he corresponds with the "Jupiter Tonans" of the Romans, being the "prince of the power of the air," the lord of the whirlwind and the tempest, and the wielder of the thunderbolt. His most common titles are "the minister of heaven and earth," "the lord of the air," and "he who makes the tempest to rage." He is regarded as the destroyer of crops, the rooter-up of

[1] This is the position which he holds regularly in the Inscriptions of Asshurbanipal, the son of Esarhaddon. (See "Records of the Past," vol. i. pp. 58, 71, 77, 93–5, 99, 100, 103, etc.).

[2] See above, p. 43.

[3] "Records of the Past," vol. vii. p. 138.

[4] *Ibid.* vol. ix. p. 100.

[5] *Ibid.* vol. iii. p. 46; vol. v. pp. 24–26.

4

trees, the scatterer of the harvest; famine, scarcity, and even their consequence, pestilence, are assigned

to him. He is said to have in his hand a "flaming sword," with which he effects his ravages; and this "flaming sword," which probably represents lightning, seems to form his emblem on the tablets and cylinders, where it is figured as a double or triple bolt. But Vul has also a softer character; as the god of the atmosphere he gives the rain; and hence he is "the careful and beneficent chief," "the giver of abundance," and "the lord of fecundity." In this capacity, he is naturally chosen to preside over canals, the great fertilisers in Mesopotamia; and thus we find among his titles, "the lord of canals," and "the establisher of works of irrigation."[1]

VUL.

To the eight "great gods," whose functions have been here described, may be added most conveniently in this place, six goddesses. It was a general, though not a universal rule, in the Assyrian and Babylonian mythology, that each god should have a wife. From this law the heads of the respective pantheons, Il and Asshur, were exempt;[2] but otherwise almost all

[1] "Ancient Monarchies," vol. i. pp. 164, 165.

[2] In one place I observe a mention of a "goddess Assuritu" ("Records," vol. i. p. 60), who might seem to be a feminine form of Asshur. But the original reads, "Asshur va Ishtar Assuritu," which shows Assuritu to be a mere title of Ishtar. (See G. Smith's "Annals of Asshurbanipal," p. 17.)

the principal deities are united in pairs, one of whom is male and the other female. Anu has a wife called Anata or Anat, who is a pale and shadowy personage, the mere faint reflex of her husband whose name she receives, merely modified by a feminine inflection. Bil or Bel has a wife, Bilat, known to the classical writers as Beltis or Mylitta,[1] a term standing to Bil as Anat to Anu, but designating a far more substantial being. Beltis is "the mother of the gods," "the *great* goddess," "the great lady," "the queen of the lands," and "the queen of fecundity." She corresponds to the Cybele of the Phrygians, the Rhea of the Greeks, and the "Magna Mater" or "Bona Dea" of the Romans. Occasionally, she adds to this character the attributes of Bellona and even Diana, being spoken of as presiding over war and hunting. The wife of Hoa has been called Dav-kina; but the first element of the name seems now to be read more generally as Nin, while the second is rendered by *azu*.[2] Ninazu is said to have been "queen of Hades" and "the lady of the house of Death."[3] Her special office was to watch and soothe the last hours of the dying.[4] To the wife of Sin no proper name is given; but she is frequently associated with her husband under the appellation of "the great lady." The wife of Shamas is Gula or

---

[1] Herod. i. 131, 199; Hesychius ad.voc. Βηλθης.

[2] "Records of the Past," vol. ix. pp. 131, 132. Professor Sayce reads the name as Ninkigal (*Ibid.* p. 146).

[3] See Professor Sayce's note on the passage last quoted.

[4] "Records," vol. v. p. 146. Compare vol. iii. p. 141.

Annnit, who was, like Beltis, a "great goddess," but had a less distinctive character, being little more than a female Sun.   Finally, Vul had a wife called Shala or Tala, whose common title is *sarrat*, "Queen," but who is a colourless and insignificant personage.

On the second of the two great triads which hold so high a place in the Assyrian and Babylonian pantheons, there follows a group of five gods, with an unmistakably astral character.   These are Nin or Bar, Merodach or Marduk, Nergal, Ishtar, and Nebo, who correspond respectively to the planets, Saturn, Jupiter, Mars, Venus, and Mercury.

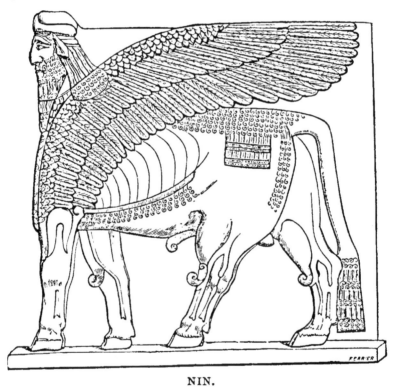

NIN.

Nin, or Bar, who presided over the most distant of the visible planets, Saturn, was more an object of worship in Assyria than in Babylonia. He has been called "the Assyrian Hercules,"[1] and in many respects resembles that hero of the classical nations. Among his titles are found, "the lord of the brave," "the warlike," "the champion," "the warrior who subdues foes," "the reducer of the disobedient," "the exterminator of rebels," "the powerful lord," "the exceeding strong god," and "he whose sword is good." He presides in a great measure both over war and hunting. Most of the Assyrian monarchs represent themselves as going out to war under his auspices, and ascribe their successes mainly to his interposition. He is especially useful to them in the subjection of rebels. He also on some occasions incites them to engage in the chase, and aids them strenuously in their encounters with wild bulls and lions.[2] It is thought that he was emblematically portrayed in the winged and human-headed bull, which forms so striking a feature in the architectural erections of the Assyrians.

As Nin was a favourite Assyrian, so Merodach was a favorite Babylonian god. From the earliest times the Babylonian monarchs placed him in the highest rank of deities, worshipping him in conjunction with Anu, Bel, and Hea, the three gods of the first triad.[3] The great temple of Babylon, known to the Greeks

---

[1] Layard, "Nineveh and Babylon," p. 214; "Records of the Past," vol. v. pp. 7, 21, 23, etc.

[2] See "Records of the Past," vol. v. p. 21.

[3] See the Inscription of Agu-kak-rimi, published in the "Records of the Past," vol. vii. p. 3, lines 5 and 6.

as the Temple of Bel,[1] was certainly dedicated to
him; and it would therefore seem that the later
Babylonians, at any rate, must have habitually applied to him the name of Bel, or "lord," which in
earlier times had designated a different member of
their pantheon. Merodach's ordinary titles are,
"the great," "the great lord," "the prince," "the
prince of the gods," and "the august god." He is
also called, "the judge," "the most ancient," "he
who judges the gods," "the eldest son of heaven,"
and in one place, "the lord of battles."[2] Occasionally, he has still higher and seemingly exclusive
designations, such as, "the great lord of eternity,"
"the king of heaven and earth," "the lord of all
beings," "the chief of the gods," and "the god of
gods."[3] But these titles seem not to be meant exclusively. He is held in considerable honour among
the Assyrians, being often coupled with Asshur,[4] or
with Asshur and Nebo,[5] as a war-god, one by whom
the kings gain victories, and obtain the destruction
of their enemies. But it is in Babylonia, and especially in the later Babylonian Empire under Nebuchadnezzar and Neriglissar, that his worship cul-
minates. It is then that all the epithets of highest
honour are accumulated upon him, and that he be-

[1] Herod. i. 181–183; Strab. xvi. p. 1049; Arrian, "Exp. Alex."
vii. 17.

[2] "Records of the Past," vol. v. p. 29.

[3] *Ibid.* vol. v. pp. 112, 119, 122; vol. ix. pp. 96, 106.

[4] "Records of the Past," vol. i. p. 20; vol. iii. pp. 53, 55; vol.
v. p. 41; vol. x. p. 53, etc.

[5] *Ibid.* vol. vii. pp. 25, 27, 45, etc.

comes an almost exclusive object of worship; it is then that we find such expressions as: "I supplicated the king of gods, the lord of lords, in Borsippa, the city of his loftiness,"[1] and "O god Merodach, great lord, lord of the house of the gods, light of the gods, father, even for thy high honor, which changeth not, a temple have I built."[2]

In his stellar character, Merodach represented the planet Jupiter, with which he was supposed to have a very intimate connection. The eighth month (Marchesvan) was dedicated to him.[3] In the second Elul he had three festivals—on the third, on the seventh, and on the sixteenth day.[4]

Nergal, who presided over the planet Mars, was essentially a war-god. His name signifies "the great man," or the "great hero;"[5] and his commonest titles are "the mighty hero," "the king of battle," "the destroyer," "the champion of the gods," and "the great brother." He "goes before" the kings in their warlike expeditions, and helps them to confound and destroy their enemies. Nor is he above lending them his assistance when they indulge in the pleasures of the chase. One of his titles is "the god of hunting,"[6] and while originally subordinated to Nin in this relation, ultimately he outstrips his rival, and becomes the especial patron of hunters and sportsmen. Asshur-bani-pal, who

[1] "Records of the Past," vol. v. p. 120. [2] *Ibid.* p. 142.
[3] *Ibid.* vol. vii. p. 169. [4] *Ibid.* pp. 159, 160 and 163.
[5] Sir Rawlinson in the Author's "Herodotus," vol. i. p. 655.
[6] Sir H. Rawlinson in the Author's "Herodotus," l. s. c.

is conspicuous among the Assyrian kings for his in-
tense love of field sports, uniformly ascribes his successes to Nergal, and does not even join with him
any other deity.   Nergal's emblem was the human-
headed and winged lion, which is usually seen, as it
were on guard, at the entrance of the royal palaces.

NERGAL.

Ishtar, who was called Nana by the Babylonians,[1]
corresponded both in name and attributes with the
Astarte of the Phœnicians and Syrians.   Like the
Greek Aphrodite and the Latin Venus, she was the
Queen of Love and Beauty, the goddess who presided
over the loves both of men and animals, and whose

[1] "Records of the Past," vol. iii. pp. 7, 10, 11, 13, 14. etc.;
vol. v. pp. 72, 83, 102, etc.

own amours were notorious. In one of the Izdubar legends, she courts that romantic individual, who however, declines her advances, reminding her that her favour had always proved fatal to those persons on whom she had previously bestowed her affections.[1] There can be little doubt that in Babylon, at any rate, she was worshipped with unchaste rites,[2] and that her cult was thus of a corrupting and debasing character. But besides and beyond this soft and sensual aspect, Ishtar had a further and nobler one. She corresponded, not to Venus only, but also to Bellona; being called "the goddess of war and battle," "the queen of victory," "she who arranges battles," and "she who defends from attack." The Assyrian kings very generally unite her with Asshur, in the accounts which they give of their expeditions;[3] speaking of their forces as those which Asshur and Ishtar had committed to their charge; of their battles as fought in the service of Asshur and Ishtar and of their triumphs as the result of Asshur and Ishtar exalting them above their enemies. Ishtar had also some general titles of a lofty but vague character; she was called, "the fortunate," "the happy," "the great goddess," "the mistress of heaven and earth," and "the queen of all the gods and goddesses." In her stellar aspect, she presided over the planet Venus; and the sixth month, Elul, was dedicated to her.[4]

Nebo, the last of the five planetary deities, presided

[1] "Records of the Past," vol. ix. pp. 125–128.
[2] See Herod. i. 199; of Baruch vi. 43, and Strabo, xvi. p. 1058.
[3] "Records of the Past," vol. i. pp. 69–86; vol. iii. p. 45, etc.
[4] *Ibid.* vol. vii. p. 169.

over Mercury. It was his special function to have under his charge learning and knowledge. He is called "the god who possesses intelligence,"[1] "he who hears from afar," "he who teaches," and "he who teaches and instructs."[2] The tablets of the royal library at Nineveh are said to contain "the wisdom of Nebo."[3] He is also, like Mercury, "the minister of the gods," though scarcely their messenger, an office which belongs to Paku. At the same time, as has often been remarked,[4] Nebo has, like many other of the Assyrian and Babylonian gods, a number of general titles, implying divine power, which, if they had belonged to him alone, would have seemed to prove him the supreme deity. He is "the lord of lords, who has no equal in power," "the supreme chief," "the sustainer," "the supporter," "the ever ready," "the guardian of heaven and earth," "the lord of the constellations," "the holder of the sceptre of power," "he who grants to kings the sceptre of royalty for the governance of their people." It is chiefly by his omission from many lists, and by his humble place,[5] when he is mentioned together with the really "great gods," that we are assured of his occupying a (comparatively speaking) low position in the general pantheon.

1 "Records of the Past," vol. v. pp. 113, 122, etc.

2 "Ancient Monarchies," vol. i. p. 177.

3 "Records of the Past," vol. i. p. 58.

4 Sir H. Rawlinson in the Author's "Herodotus," vol. i. p. 661; "Ancient Monarchies," l. s. c.

5 Nebo's place varies commonly from the fifth to the thirteenth,

The planetary gods had in most instances a female complement. Nebo was closely associated with a goddess called Urmit or Tasmit, Nergal with one called Laz, and Merodach with Zirpanit or Zirbanit. Nin, the son of Bel and Beltis, is sometimes made the husband of his mother,[1] but otherwise has no female counterpart. Ishtar is sometimes coupled with Nebo in a way that might suggest her being his wife,[2] if it were not that that position is certainly occupied by Urmit.

Among other Assyrian and Babylonian deities may be mentioned Nusku, a god assigned a high rank by Asshur-bani-pal;[3] Makhir, the goddess of dreams,[4] Paku, the divine messenger,[5] Laguda, the god of a town call Kisik;[6] Zamal, Turda, Ishkara, Malik, deities invoked in curses;[7] Zicum, a primeval goddess, said to be "the mother of Anu; and the gods,"[8] Dakan,[9] perhaps Dagon, Martu, Zira, Idak, Kurrikh, etc. Many other strange names also occur, but either rarely, or in a connection which is thought to indicate that they are local appellations of some of the

and is generally about the seventh. Nebuchadnezzar, however, puts him third. ("Records of the Past," vol. v. p. 122.)

[1] "Ancient Monarchies," vol. i. p. 169.

[2] "Ancient Monarchies," vol. i. p. 176.

[3] "Records of the Past," vol. i. pp. 57, 58, 71, 77, 94, 95, etc.: vol. ix. pp. 45, 61, etc.

[4] *Ibid.* vol. ix. p. 152.

[5] *Ibid.* vol. v. p. 165.

[6] *Ibid.* vol. ix. pp. 3 and 15.

[7] *Ibid.* p. 101.

[8] *Ibid.* p. 146, and note.

[9] *Ibid.* vol. iii. p. 40; vol. v. p. 117; vol. vii. pp. 11, 27, etc.

well-known deities. No more need be said of these personages, since the general character of the religion is but little affected by the belief in gods who played so very insignificant a part in the system.

The Assyrians and Babylonians worshipped their gods in shrines or chapels of no very great size, to which, however, was frequently attached a lofty tower, built in stages, which were sometimes as many as seven.[1] The tower could be ascended by steps on the outside, and was usually crowned by a small chapel. The gods were represented by images, which were either of stone or metal, and which bore the human form, excepting in two instances. Nin and Nergal were portrayed, as the Jews, perhaps, portrayed their cherubim, by animal forms of great size and grandeur, having human heads and huge outstretched wings.[2] There was nothing hideous or even grotesque about the representations of the Assyrian gods. The object aimed at was to fill the spectator with feelings of awe and reverence; and the figures have, in fact, universally, an appearance of calm placid strength and majesty, which is most solemn and impressive.

The gods were worshipped, as generally in the ancient world, by prayer, praise, and sacrifice. Prayer was offered both for oneself and for others. The "sinfulness of sin" was deeply felt, and the Divine anger deprecated with much earnestness. "O! my

[1] As at Borsippa (Birs-i-Nimrod), where a portion of each stage remains.

[2] Ezek. x. 8–22.

Lord," says one suppliant, "my sins are many, my trespasses are great; and the wrath of the gods has plagued me with disease, and sickness, and sorrow. I fainted, but no one stretched forth his hand; I groaned, but no one drew nigh. I cried aloud, but no one heard. O Lord, do not Thou abandon thy servant. In the waters of the great storm, do Thou lay hold of his hand. The sins which he has committed, do Thou turn to righteousness."[1] Special intercession was made for the Assyrian kings. The gods were besought to grant them "length of days, a strong sword, extended years of glory, pre-eminence among monarchs, and an enlargement of the bounds of their empire."[2] It is thought that their happiness in a future state was also prayed for.[3] Praise was even more frequent than prayer. The gods were addressed under their various titles, and their benefits to mankind commemorated. "O Fire!" we read on one tablet,[4] "Great Lord, who art exalted above all the earth! O! noble son of heaven, exalted above all the earth. O Fire, with thy bright flame, thou dost produce light in the dark house! Of all things that can be named, thou dost create the fabric; of bronze and of lead, thou art the melter; of silver and of gold, thou art the refiner; of . . . thou art the purifier. Of the wicked man, in the night-time,

---

[1] "Records of the Past," vol iii. p. 136.

[2] *Ibid.* p. 133.

[3] Fox Talbot in the "Transactions of the Society of Biblical Archæology," vol. i. p. 107.

[4] "Records of the Past," vol. iii. pp. 137, 138.

thou dost repel the assault; but the man who serves his God, thou wilt give him light for his actions." Sacrifice almost always accompanied prayer and praise. Every day in the year seems to have been sacred to some deity or deities, and some sacrifice or other was offered every day by the monarch,[1] who thus set an example to his subjects, which we may be sure they were not slow to follow. The principal sacrificial animals were bulls, oxen, sheep, and gazelles.[2] Libations of wine were also a part of the recognised worship,[3] and offerings might be made of anything valuable.

It is an interesting question how far the Assyrians and Babylonians entertained any confident expectation of a future life, and, if so, what view they took of it. That the idea did not occupy a prominent place in their minds ; that there was a contrast in this respect between them and the people of Egypt, is palpable from the very small number of passages in which anything like an allusion to a future state of existence has been detected. Still, there certainly seem to be places in which the continued existence of the dead is spoken of, and where the happiness of the good and the wretchedness of the wicked in the future state are indicated. It has been already noticed, that in one passage the happiness of the king in another world seems to be prayed for. In two or

[1] See the fragment of a Calendar published in the " Records of the Past," vol. vii. pp. 159–168.

[2] *Ibid.* pp. 137, 159, and 161 ; " Ancient Monarchies," vol ii. p. 271.

[3] " Records of the Past," vol. iii. p. 124 ; vol. vii. p. 140.

three others, prayer is offered for a departing soul in terms like the following : " May the sun give him life, and Merodach grant him an abode of happiness," [1] or, " To the sun, the greatest of the gods, may he ascend ; and may the sun, the greatest of the gods, receive his soul into his holy hands." [2] The nature of the happiness enjoyed may be gathered from occasional notices, where the soul is represented as clad in a white radiant garment,[3] as dwelling in the presence of the gods, and as partaking of celestial food in the abode of blessedness. On the other hand, Hades, the receptacle of the wicked after death, is spoken of as " the abode of darkness and famine," the place " where earth is men's food, and their nourishment clay ; where light is not seen, but in darkness they dwell ; where ghosts, like birds, flutter their wings, and on the door and the doorposts the dust lies undisturbed." [4] Different degrees of sinfulness seem to meet with different and appropriate punishments. There is one place—apparently, a penal fire—reserved for unfaithful wives and husbands, and for youths who have dishonored their bodies. Thus it would appear that M. Lenormant was mistaken when he said, that, though the Assyrians recognised a place of departed spirits, yet it

[1] " Transactions of the Society of Biblical Archæology," vol. ii. p. 32.

[2] *Ibid.* p. 31.

[3] " Records of the Past," vol. iii. p. 135.

[4] " Transactions," etc., vol. i. p. 113.

was one "in which there was no trace of a distinction of rewards and punishments." [1]

The superstitions of the Assyrians and Babylonians were numerous and strange. They believed in charms of various kinds ; [2] in omens, [3] in astrology, in spells, and in a miraculous power inherent in an object which they called "the Mamit." What the Mamit was is quite uncertain. [4] According to the native belief, it had descended from heaven, and was a "treasure," a "priceless jewel," infinitely more valuable than anything else upon the earth. It was ordinarily kept in a temple, but was sometimes brought to the bedside of a sick person, with the object of driving out the evil spirits to whom his disease was owing, and of so recovering him.

Among the sacred legends of the Babylonians and Assyrians the following were the most remarkable. They believed that at a remote date, before the creation of the world, there had been war in heaven. Seven spirits, created by Anu to be his messengers, took counsel together and resolved to revolt. "Against high heaven, the dwelling-place of Anu the king, they plotted evil," and unexpectedly made

[1] "Records of the Past," vol. i. p. 143.

[2] *Ibid.* vol. iii. p. 142.

[3] Among the remains of Assyrian and Babylonian literature are tables of omens derived from dreams, from births, from an inspection of the hand, or of the entrails of animals, and from the objects a traveller meets with on his journey. Dogs alone furnish eighteen omens (*Ibid.*, vol. v. pp. 169–170).

[4] See a paper by Mr. Fox Talbot in the "Transactions of the Society of Biblical Archæology," vol. ii. pp. 35–42.

a fierce attack. The moon, the sun, and Vul, the god of the atmosphere, withstood them, and after a fearful struggle beat them off.[1] There was then peace for a while. But once more, at a later date, a fresh revolt broke out. The hosts of heaven were assembled together, in number five thousand, and were engaged in singing a psalm of praise to Anu, when suddenly discord arose. " With a loud cry of contempt" a portion of the angelic choir " broke up the holy song," uttering wicked blasphemies, and so "spoiling, confusing, confounding the hymn of praise." Asshur was asked to put himself at their head, but " refused to go forth with them." [2] Their leader, who is unnamed, took the form of a dragon, and in that shape contended with the god Bel, who proved victorious in the combat, and slew his adversary by means of a thunderbolt, which he flung into the creature's open mouth.[3] Upon this, the entire host of the wicked angels took to flight, and was driven to the abode of the seven spirits of evil, where they were forced to remain, their return to heaven being prohibited. In their room man was created.[4]

The Chaldæan legend of creation, according to Berosus, was as follows :—

"In the beginning all was darkness and water, and therein were generated monstrous animals of

[1] " Records of the Past," vol. v. pp. 163–166.
[2] *Ibid.* vol. vii. pp. 127, 128.
[3] *Ibid.* vol. ix. pp. 137–139.
[4] *Ibid.* vol. vii. p. 127.

strange and peculiar forms. There were men with
two wings, and some even with four, and with two
faces; and others with two heads, a man's and a woman's, on one body; and there were men with the
heads and horns of goats, and men with hoofs like
horses; and some with the upper parts of a man
joined to the lower parts of a horse, like centaurs;
and there were bulls with human heads, dogs with
four bodies and with fishes' tails; men and horses
with dogs' heads; creatures with the heads and
bodies of horses, but with the tails of fish;
and other animals mixing the forms of various
beasts. Moreover, there were monstrous fishes and
reptiles and serpents, and divers other creatures,
which had borrowed something from each other's
shapes, of all which the likenesses are still preserved
in the temple of Belus. A woman ruled them all,
by name Omorka, which is in Chaldee Thalath, and
in Greek Thalassa (or 'the sea'). Then Belus appeared, and split the woman in twain; and of the
one half of her he made the heaven, and of the other
half the earth; and the beasts that were in her he
caused to perish. And he split the darkness, and divided the heaven and the earth asunder, and put the
world in order, and the animals that could not bear
the light perished. Belus, upon this, seeing that the
earth was desolate, yet teeming with productive powers, commanded one of the gods to cut off his head,
and to mix the blood which flowed forth with earth,
and form men therewith, and beasts that could bear
the light. So man was made, and was intelligent,

being a partaker of the Divine wisdom. Likewise Belus made the stars, and the sun and the moon, and the five planets."[1]

The only native account which has been discovered in part resembles this, but in many respects is different. So far as at present deciphered, it runs thus:—

"When the upper region was not yet called heaven, and the lower region was not yet called earth, and the abyss of Hades had not yet opened its arms, then the chaos of waters gave birth to all; and the waters were gathered into one place. Men dwelt not as yet together; no animals as yet wandered about; nor as yet had the gods been born; not as yet had their names been uttered, or their attributes [fixed]. Then were born the gods Lakhmu and Lakhamu; they were born and grew up . . . . Asshur and Kisshur were born and lived through many days . . . . . Anu (was born next).

*   *   *   *   *

"He (Anu?) constructed dwellings for the great gods; he fixed the constellations, whose figures were like animals. He made the year into portions; he divided it; twelve months he established, with their constellations, three by three. And from among the days of the year he appointed festivals; he made dwellings for the planets, for their rising and for their setting. And, that nothing should go wrong, nor come to a stand, he placed along with them the

[1] Berosus ap. Euseb. "Chron. Can." i. 2; Syncell. "Chronographia," vol. i. p. 53.

dwellings of Bel and Hea; and he opened great gates on all sides, making strong the portals on the left and on the right. Moreover, in the centre he placed luminaries. The moon he set on high to circle through the night, and made it wander all the night until the dawning of the day. Each month without fail it brought together festal assemblies; in the beginning of the month, at the rising of the night, shooting forth its horns to illuminate the heavens, and on the seventh day a holy day appointing, and commanding on that day a cessation from all business. And he (Anu) set the sun in his place in the horizon of heaven." [1]

The following is the Chaldæan account of the Deluge, as rendered from the original by the late Mr. George Smith: [2]—

" Hea spake to me and said:—'Son of Ubaratutu, make a ship after this fashion . . . . for I destroy the sinners and life . . . . and cause to enter in all the seed of life, that thou mayest preserve them. The ship which thou shalt make, ... cubits shall be the measure of the length thereof, and . . . . cubits the measure of the breadth and height thereof; and into the deep thou shalt launch it.' I understood, and said to Hea, my Lord—'Hea, my Lord, this which Thou commandest me, I will perform:

[1] " Records of the Past," vol. ix. pp. 117–118.

[2] Mr. Smith's paper, read on Dec. 3, 1872, was first published in the "Transactions of the Society of Biblical Archæology," in 1874. It was afterwards revised, and republished in the " Records of the Past," vol. xii. pp. 135–141. The translation is taken mainly from this second version.

[though I be derided] both by young and old, it shall be done.' Hea opened his mouth, and spake— 'This shalt thou say to them . . . . (hiatus of six lines) . . . . and enter thou into the ship, and shut to the door; and bring into the midst of it thy grain, and thy furniture, and thy goods, thy wealth, thy servants, thy female slaves and thy young men. And I will gather to thee the beasts of the field, and the animals, and I will bring them to thee; and they shall be enclosed within thy door.' Hasisadra his mouth opened and spake, and said to Hea, his Lord—'There was not upon the earth a man who could make the ship . . . . strong [planks] I brought . . . . on the fifth day . . . . in its circuit fourteen measures [it measured]; in its sides fourteen measures it measured . . . . and upon it I placed its roof and closed [the door]. On the sixth day I embarked in it: on the seventh I examined it without: on the eighth I examined it within; planks against the influx of the waters I placed: where I saw rents and holes, I added what was required. Three measures of bitumen I poured over the outside: three measures of bitumen I poured over the inside . . . . (five lines obscure and mutilated). . . . . Wine in receptacles I collected, like the waters of a river; also [food], like the dust of the earth, I collected in boxes [and stored up.] And Shamas the material of the ship completed [and made it] strong. And the reed oars of the ship I caused them to bring [and place] above and below. . . . . All I possessed of silver, all I possessed of gold, all I possessed of the

seed of life, I caused to ascend into the ship. All
my male servants, all my female servants, all the
beasts of the field, all the animals, all the sons of the
people, I caused to go up. A flood Shamas made,
and thus he spake in the night: 'I will cause it to
rain from heaven heavily. Enter into the midst of
the ship, and shut thy door.'"

The command of Shamas is obeyed, and then
"The raging of a storm in the morning arose, from
the horizon of heaven extending far and wide. Vul
in the midst of it thundered: Nebo and Saru went
in front: the throne-bearers sped over mountains
and plains: the destroyer, Nergal, overturned: Ninip
went in front and cast down: the spirits spread
abroad destruction: in their fury they swept the
earth: the flood of Vul reached to heaven. The
bright earth to a waste was turned: the storm o'er
its surface swept: from the face of the earth was life
destroyed: the strong flood that had whelmed mankind reached to heaven: brother saw not brother;
the flood did not spare the people. Even in heaven
the gods feared the tempest, and sought refuge in
the abode of Anu. Like dogs the gods crouched
down, and cowered together. Spake Ishtar, like a
child—uttered the great goddess her speech: 'When
the world to corruption turned, then I in the presence of the gods prophesied evil. When I in the
presence of the gods prophesied evil, then to evil
were devoted all my children. I, the mother, have
given birth to my people, and lo! now like the
young of fishes they fill the sea.' The gods were

weeping for the spirits with her; the gods in their seats were sitting in lamentation; covered were their lips on account of the coming evil. Six days and nights passed; the wind, the flood, the storm overwhelmed. On the seventh day, in its course was calmed the storm; and all the tempest, which had destroyed like an earthquake, was quieted. The flood He caused to dry; the wind and the deluge ended. I beheld the tossing of the sea, and mankind all turned to corruption; like reeds the corpses floated. I opened the window, and the light broke over my face. It passed. I sat down and wept; over my face flowed my tears. I saw the shore at the edge of the sea; for twelve measures the land rose. To the country of Nizir went the ship: the mountain of Nizir stopped the ship: to pass over it was not able. The first day and the second day the mountain of Nizir, the same; the third day and the fourth day the mountain of Nizir, the same; the fifth and sixth the mountain of Nizir, the same; in the course of the seventh day I sent out a dove, and it left. The dove went to and fro, and a resting-place it did not find, and it returned. I sent forth a swallow, and it left; the swallow went to and fro, and a resting-place it did not find, and it returned. I sent forth a raven, and it left; the raven went, and the corpses on the waters it saw, and it did eat: it swam, and wandered away, and returned not. I sent the animals forth to the four winds: I poured out a libation: I built an altar on the peak of the mountain: seven jugs of wine I took; at the bottom

I placed reeds, pines, and spices. The gods collected
to the burning: the gods collected to the good burning. Like *sumpe* (?) over the sacrifice they gathered.'"

One more example must conclude our specimens
of the legends current among the Assyrians and
Babylonians in ancient times. As the preceding
passage is myth based upon history, the concluding
one shall be taken from that portion of Assyrian lore
which is purely and wholly imaginative. The
descent of Ishtar to Hades, perhaps in search of
Tammuz, is related as follows[1] :—

"To the land of Hades, the land of her desire,
Ishtar, daughter of the Moon-god Sin, turned her
mind. The daughter of Sin fixed her mind to go to
the House where all meet, the dwelling of the god
Iskalla, to the house which men enter, but cannot
depart from—the road which men travel, but never
retrace—the abode of darkness and of famine, where
earth is their food, their nourishment clay—where
light is not seen, but in darkness they dwell--where
ghosts, like birds, flutter their wings, and on the
door and the door-posts the dust lies undisturbed.

"When Ishtar arrived at the gate of Hades, to
the keeper of the gate a word she spake: 'O keeper
of the entrance, open thy gate! Open thy gate, I
say again, that I may enter in! If thou openest

[1] The translation of Mr. Fox Talbot, as given in the "Transactions of the Society of Biblical Archæology," vol. iii. pp. 119–124,
and again in "Records of the Past," vol. i. pp. 143–149, is here
followed.

not thy gate, if I do not enter in, I will assault the door, the gate I will break down, I will attack the entrance, I will split open the portals. I will raise the dead, to be the devourers of the living! Upon the living the dead shall prey.' Then the porter opened his mouth and spake, and thus he said to great Ishtar: 'Stay, lady, do not shake down the door; I will go and inform Queen Nin-ki-gal.' So the porter went in and to Nin-ki-gal said: 'These curses thy sister Ishtar utters; yea, she blasphemes thee with fearful curses.' And Nin-ki-gal, hearing the words, grew pale, like a flower when cut from the stem; like the stalk of a reed, she shook. And she said, 'I will cure her rage—I will speedily cure her fury. Her curses I will repay. Light up consuming flames! Light up a blaze of straw! Be her doom with the husbands who left their wives; be her doom with the wives who forsook their lords; be her doom with the youths of dishonored lives. Go, porter, and open the gate for her; but strip her, as some have been stripped ere now.' The porter went and opened the gate. 'Lady of Tiggaba, enter,' he said: 'Enter. It is permitted. The Queen of Hades to meet thee comes.' So the first gate let her in, but she was stopped, and there the great crown was taken from her head. 'Keeper, do not take off from me the crown that is on my head.' 'Excuse it, lady, the Queen of the Land insists upon its removal.' The next gate let her in, but she was stopped, and there the ear-rings were taken from her ears. 'Keeper, do not take off from me the ear-rings from my ears.' 'Excuse it, lady, the Queen of the Land insists upon their removal.' The third gate let her in, but she was stopped, and there the precious stones were taken from her head. 'Keeper, do not take off from me the gems that adorn my head.' 'Excuse it, lady, the Queen of the Land insists upon their removal.' The fourth gate let her in, but she was stopped, and there the small jewels were taken from her brow. 'Keeper, do not take off from me the small jewels that deck my brow.' 'Excuse it, lady, the Queen of the Land insists upon their removal.' The fifth gate let her in, but she was stopped, and there the girdle was taken from her waist. 'Keeper, do not take off from me the girdle that girds my waist.' 'Excuse it, lady, the Queen of the Land insists upon its removal.' The sixth gate let her in, but she was stopped, and there the gold rings were taken from her hands and feet. 'Keeper, do not take off from me the gold rings of my hands and feet.' 'Excuse it, lady, the Queen of the Land insists upon their removal.' The seventh gate let her in, but she was stopped, and there the last garment was taken from her body. 'Keeper, do not take off, I pray, the last garment from my body.' 'Excuse it, lady, the Queen of the Land insists upon its removal.'

"After that Mother Ishtar had descended into Hades, Nin-ki-gal saw and derided her to her face. Then Ishtar lost her reason, and heaped curses upon the other. Nin-ki-gal hereupon opened her mouth, and spake: 'Go, Namtar, ... and bring

her out for punishment, . . . afflict her with disease
of the eye, the side, the feet, the heart, the head'
(some lines effaced) . . . .

"The Divine messenger of the gods lacerated his
face before them. The assembly of the gods was
full. . . . The Sun came, along with the Moon, his
father, and weeping he spake thus unto Hea, the
king: 'Ishtar has descended into the earth, and has
not risen again; and ever since the time that Mother
Ishtar descended into hell, ... the master has
ceased from commanding; the slave has ceased from
obeying.' Then the god Hea in the depth of his
mind formed a design; he modelled, for her escape,
the figure of a man of clay. 'Go to save her,
Phantom, present thyself at the portal of Hades;
the seven gates of Hades will all open before thee;
Nin-ki-gal will see thee, and take pleasure because
of thee. When her mind has grown calm, and her
anger has worn itself away, awe her with the names
of the great gods! Then prepare thy frauds! Fix
on deceitful tricks thy mind! Use the chiefest of
thy tricks! Bring forth fish out of an empty vessel!
That will astonish Nin-ki-gal, and to Ishtar she will
restore her clothing. The reward—a great reward—
for these things shall not fail. Go, Phantom, save
her, and the great assembly of the people shall crown
thee! Meats, the best in the city, shall be thy food!
Wine, the most delicious in the city, shall be thy
drink! A royal palace shall be thy dwelling, a
throne of state shall be thy seat! Magician and
conjuror shall kiss the hem of thy garment!'

" Nin-ki-gal opened her mouth and spake; to her messenger, Namtar, commands she gave: 'Go, Namtar, the Temple of Justice adorn! Deck the images! Deck the altars! Bring out Anunnak, and let him take his seat on a throne of gold! Pour out for Ishtar the water of life; from my realms let her depart.' Namtar obeyed; he adorned the Temple; decked the images, decked the altars; brought out Anunnak, and let him take his seat on a throne of gold; poured out for Ishtar the water of life, and suffered her to depart. Then the first gate let her out, and gave her back the garment of her form. The next gate let her out, and gave her back the jewels for her hands and feet. The third gate let her out, and gave her back the girdle for her waist. The fourth gate let her out, and gave her back the small gems she had worn upon her brow. The fifth gate let her out, and gave her back the precious stones that had been upon her head. The sixth gate let her out, and gave her back the ear-rings that were taken from her ears. And the seventh gate let her out, and gave her back the crown she had carried on her head."

So ends this curious legend, and with it the limits of our space require that we should terminate this notice of the religion of the Assyrians and Babylonians.

CHAPTER III.

THE RELIGION OF THE ANCIENT IRANIANS.

'Αριστοτελης φησι δυο κατ' αυτους ειναι αρχας, αγαθον δαιμονα και κακον δαιμονα.—Diog. *Laert. Proem*, p. 2.

THE Iranians were in ancient times the dominant race throughout the entire tract lying between the Suliman mountains and the Pamir steppe on the one hand, and the great Mesopotamian valley on the other. Intermixed in portions of the tract with a Cushite or Nigritic, and in others with a Turanian element, they possessed, nevertheless, upon the whole, a decided preponderance; and the tract itself has been known as "Ariana," or "Iran," at any rate from the time of Alexander the Great to the present day![1] The region is one in which extremes are brought into sharp contrast, and forced on human observation, the summers being intensely hot, and the winters piercingly cold, the more favoured portions luxuriantly fertile, the remainder an arid and frightful desert. If, as seems to be now generally thought

[1] Strabo, who is the earliest of extant writers to use "Ariana" in this broad sense, probably obtained the term from the contemporaries of Alexander. It was certainly used by Apollodorus of Artemita (ab. B. c. 130).

77

by the best informed and deepest investigators,[1] the
light of primeval relation very early faded away in
Asia, and religions there were in the main elaborated
out of the working upon the circumstances of his environment, of that "religious faculty" wherewith
God had endowed mankind, we might expect that in
this peculiar region a peculiar religion should develop
itself—a religion of strong antitheses and sharp con-
trasts, unlike that of such homogeneous tracts as the
Nile valley and the Mesopotamian plain, where cli-
mate was almost uniform, and a monotonous fertility
spread around universal abundance. The fact answers to our natural anticipation. At a time which
it is difficult to date, but which those best skilled in
Iranian antiquities are inclined to place before the
birth of Moses,[2] there grew up, in the region whereof
we are speaking, a form of religion marked by very
special and unusual features, very unlike the religions
of Egypt and Assyria, a thing quite *sui generis*, one
very worthy of the attention of those who are inter-
ested in the past history of the human race, and
more especially of such as wish to study the history
of religions.

Ancient tradition associates this religion with the
name of Zoroaster. Zoroaster, or Zarathrustra, according to the native spelling,[3] was, by one account,[4]
a Median king who conquered Babylon about B. C.

[1] See Max Müller, "Introduction to the Science of Religion,"
Lecture I. pp. 40, 41.

[2] Haug, "Essays on the Religion, etc., of the Parsees," p. 255.

[3] See "Zendavesta," *passim.*

[4] Berosus ap. Syncell. "Chronographia," p. 147.

2458. By another, which is more probable, and which rests, moreover, on better authority, he was a Bactrian,[1] who, at a date not quite so remote, came forward in the broad plain of the middle Oxus to instil into the minds of his countrymen the doctrines and precepts of a new religion. Claiming divine inspiration, and professing to hold from time to time direct conversation with the Supreme Being, he delivered his revelations in a mythical form, and obtained their general acceptance as divine by the Bactrian people. His religion gradually spread from "happy Bactra," "Bactra of the lofty banner,"[2] first to the neighbouring countries, and then to all the numerous tribes of the Iranians, until at last it became the established religion of the mighty empire of Persia, which, in the middle of the sixth century before our era, established itself on the ruins of the Assyrian and Babylonian kingdoms, and shortly afterwards overran and subdued the ancient monarchy of the Pharaohs. In Persia it maintained its ground, despite the shocks of Grecian and Parthian conquest, until Mohammedan intolerance drove it out at the point of the sword, and forced it to seek a refuge further east, in the peninsula of Hindustan. Here it still continues, in Guzerat and in Bombay, the creed of that ingenious and intelligent people known to Anglo-Indians—and may we not say to Englishmen generally?—as Parsees.

[1] Hermipp. ap. Arnob. "Adv. Gentes," i. 52; Justin, i. 1; Amm. Marc. xxiii. 6; Moses Choren. "Hist. Armen." i. 5.

[2] "Vendidad," Farg. ii. s. 7.

The religion of the Parsees is contained in a volume of some size, which has received the name of " the Zendavesta." [1]   Subjected for the last fifty years to the searching analysis of first-rate orientalists— Burnouf, Westergaard, Brockhaus, Spiegel, Haug, Windischmann, Hubschmann—this work has been found to belong in its various parts to very different dates, and to admit of being so dissected [2] as to reveal to us, not only what are the tenets of the modern Parsees, but what was the earliest form of that religion whereof theirs is the remote and degenerate descendant. Signs of a great antiquity are found to attach to the language of certain rhythmical compositions, called Gathas or hymns; and the religious ideas contained in these are found to be at once harmonious, and also of a simpler and more primitive character than those contained in the rest of the volume.   From the Gathas chiefly, but also to some extent from other, apparently very ancient, portions of the Zendavesta, the characteristics of the early Iranian religion have been drawn out by various scholars, particularly by Dr. Martin Haug; and it is from the labours of these writers, in the main,

[1] Anquetil Duperron introduced the sacred book of the Parsees to the knowledge of Europeans under this name; and the word thus introduced can scarcely be now displaced. Otherwise "Avesta-Zend" might be recommended as the more proper title. " Avesta" means "text," and "Zend" means "comment." "Avesta u Zend," or "Text and Comment" is the proper title, which is then contracted into "Avesta-Zend."

[2] Haug, "Essays," pp. 136–138; Max Muller, "Introduction to the Science of Religion," pp. 26–29.

that we shall be content to draw our picture of the religion in question.

The most striking feature of the religion, and that which is generally allowed to be its leading characteristic, is the assertion of Dualism. By Dualism we mean the belief in two original uncreated principles, a principle of good and a principle of evil. This creed was not perhaps contained in the teaching of Zoroaster himself,[1] but it was developed at so early a date[2] out of that teaching, that in treating generally of the Iranian religion we must necessarily regard Dualism as a part of it. The Iranians of historic times held that from all eternity there had existed two mighty and rival beings, the authors of all other existences, who had been engaged in a perpetual contest, each seeking to injure, baffle, and in every way annoy and thwart the other. Both principles were real persons, possessed of will, intelligence, power, consciousness, and other personal qualities. To the one they gave the name of Ahura-Mazda, to the other that of Augro-Mainyus.

Here let us pause for a moment, and consider the import of these two names. Names of deities, as Professor Max Müller has well pointed out,[3] are among the most interesting of studies; and a proper understanding of their meaning throws frequently

[1] See the Author's "Ancient Monarchies," vol. iii. pp. 104, 105.

[2] The Second Fargard of the "Vendidad," which from internal evidence may be pronounced earlier than B.C. 800, is as strongly Dualistic as any other portion of the volume.

[3] "Introduction to the Science of Religion," Lecture III. pp. 171 *et seqq.*

very considerable light on the nature and character of a religion. Now, Ahura-Mazda is a word composed of three elements: "Ahura," "maz," "da." The first of these is properly an adjective, signifying, "living;" it corresponds to "asura" in Sanskrit, and like that passes from an adjectival to a substantival force, and is used for "living being," especially for living beings superior to man. Perhaps it may be best expressed in English by the word "spirit," only that we must not regard absolute immateriality as implied in it. "Maz" is cognate to the "maj" in major, and the "mag" or "meg" in "magnus" and μέγας; it is an intensitive, and means "much." "Da" or "dao" is a word of a double meaning; it is a participle, or verbal adjective, and signifies either "giving" or "knowing," being connected with the Latin "do," "dare" (Greek δίδωμι), "to give," and with the Greek δαῆναι, δαῆμων, "to know," "knowing." The entire word, "Ahura-Mazda," thus means either, "the much-knowing spirit," or the "much-giving spirit," the "all-bountiful," or "the all-wise." [1]

Angro-Mainyus contains two elements only, an adjective and a substantive. "Angro" is akin to "niger," and so to "negro;" it means simply "black" or "dark." "Mainyus," a substantive, is the exact equivalent of the Latin "mens," and the Greek μένος. It means "mind," "intelligence." Thus Angro-Mainyus is the "black or dark intelligence."

[1] See Haug, "Essays," p. 33; Brockhaus, "Vendidad-Sade," pp. 347 and 385: and Sir H. Rawlinson, "Persian Vocabulary," ad voc. "Auramazda."

Thus the names themselves sufficiently indicated to those who first used them the nature of the two beings. Ahura-Mazda was the "all-bountiful, all-wise, living being" or "spirit," who stood at the head of all that was good and lovely, beautiful and delightful. Angro-Mainyus was the "dark and gloomy intelligence," that had from the first been Ahura-Mazda's enemy, and was bent on thwarting and vexing him. And with these fundamental notions agreed all that the sacred books taught concerning either being. Ahura-Mazda was declared to be "the creator of life, the earthly and the spiritual;" he had made "the celestial bodies," "earth, water, and trees," "all good creatures," and "all good, true things." He was "good," "holy," "pure," "true," "the holy god," "the holiest," "the essence of truth," "the father of truth," "the best being of all," "the master of purity." Supremely happy, he possessed every blessing, "health, wealth, virtue, wisdom, immortality."[1] From him came all good to man—on the pious and the righteous he bestowed, not only earthly advantages, but precious spiritual gifts, truth, devotion, "the good mind," and everlasting happiness; and, as he rewarded the good, so he also punished the bad, although this was an aspect in which he was but seldom contemplated.

[1] The expressions in inverted commas are all taken from Haug's translations of the *Yasna* given in his "Essays." The exact place of each is noted in the Author's "Ancient Monarchies," vol. iii. p. 96.

Angro-Mainyus, on the other hand, was the creator and upholder of everything that was evil. Opposed to Ahura-Mazda from the beginning, he had been engaged in a perpetual warfare with him. Whatever good thing Ahura-Mazda had created, Angro-Mainyus had corrupted and ruined it.[1] Moral and physical evils were alike at his disposal. He could blast the earth with barrenness, or make it produce thorns, thistles, and poisonous plants; his were the earthquake, the storm, the plague of hail, the thunderbolt; he could cause disease and death, sweep off a nation's flocks and herds by murrain, or depopulate a continent by pestilence; ferocious wild beasts, serpents, toads, mice, hornets, musquitoes, were his creation; he had invented and introduced into the world the sins of witchcraft, murder, unbelief, cannibalism; he excited wars and tumults, continually stirred up the bad against the good, and laboured by every possible expedient to make vice triumph over virtue. Ahura-Mazda could exercise no control over him; the utmost that he could do was to keep a perpetual watch upon his rival, and seek to baffle and defeat him. This he was not always able to do; despite his best endeavours, Angro-Mainyus was not unfrequently victorious.

The two great beings who thus divided between them the empire of the universe, were neither of them content to be solitary. Each had called into existence a number of inferior spirits, who acknowledged

[1] See the Second Fargard of the "Vendidad," which is given at length in the above-mentioned work, vol. iii. pp. 238–240.

their sovereignty, fought on their side, and sought to execute their behests. At the head of the good spirits subject to Ahura-Mazda stood a band of six dignified with the title of Amesha-Spentas, or "Immortal Holy Ones," the chief assistants of the Principle of Good both in counsel and in action. These were Vohu-mano, or Bahman, the "Good Mind"; Asha-vahista, or Ardibehesht, "the Highest Truth;" Khshathra-vairya, or Shahravar, the genius of wealth: Spenta-Armaiti (Island-armat), the genius of the Earth: Haurvatat (Khordad), the genius of Health: and Ameretat (Amerdat), the genius of Immortality.[1] In direct antithesis to these stood the band, likewise one of six, which formed the council and chief support of Angro-Mainyus, namely, Akomano, "the Bad Mind": Indra, the god of storms: Saurva: Naonhaitya: Taric: and Zaric.[2] Besides these leading spirits there was marshalled on either side an innumerable host of lesser and subordinate ones, called respectively *ahuras* and *devas*, who constituted the armies or attendants of the two great powers and were employed by them to work out their purposes. The leader of the angelic hosts, or *ahuras*, was a glorious being, called Sraosha or Serosh[3]— "the good, tall, fair Serosh," who stood in the Zoroastrian system where Michael the Archangel stands

[1] Haug, "Essays," p. 263; Pusey, "Lectures on Daniel," pp. 536, 537.

[2] Haug, l. s. c.; Windischmann, "Zoroastrische Studien," p. 59.

[3] On Serosh, see the Author's "Ancient Monarchies," vol. iii. pp. 99, 112.

in the Christian.[1] The armies of Angro-Mainyus
had no such single leader, but fought under the
orders of a number of co-equal captains, as Drukhs,
" destruction ": Aeshemo, " rapine": Daivis, " deceit ": Driwis, " poverty": and others. Offering
an uninterrupted and dogged resistance to the army
of Ahura-Mazda, they maintained the struggle on
something like equal terms, and showed no sign of
any intention to make their submission.

Neither Ahura-Mazda nor the Amesha-Spentas
were represented by the early Iranians under any
material forms. The Zoroastrian system was markedly anti-idolatrous: and the utmost that was al-

WINGED CIRCLE.

lowed the worshipper was an emblematic representation of the Supreme Being by means of a winged
circle, with which was occasionally combined an incomplete human figure, robed and wearing a tiara.

[1] It is no doubt true, as Dr. Pusey observes ("Lectures on
Daniel," p. 535), that the character of the Amesha-Spentas, and
of the other great spirits or genii of the Zendavesta, is altogether
" below that of the holy angels," and that the term "archangel,"
if applied to any of them, is "a misnomer" (*Ibid.* p. 538). But
still there is sufficient resemblance to make the comparison natural and not improper.

FOUR-WINGED FIGURE AT MURGAB.   87

A four-winged figure at Murgab, the ancient Pasar-
gadæ, is also possibly a representation of Serosh ;
but otherwise the objects of their religious regards
were not exhibited in material shapes by the early
Iranians.

Among the angelic beings reverenced by the
Iranians lower than the Amesha-Spentas, but still of
a very high rank and dignity, were Mithra, the
genius of light, early identified with the sun ; Tistrya,
the Dog-star ;[1] Airyaman, a genius presiding over
marriage ;[2] and others. Mithra was originally not
held in very high esteem ; but by degrees he was
advanced, and ultimately came to occupy a place only
a little inferior to that assigned from the first to Ahura-
Mazda. Darius, the son of Hystaspes, placed the
emblems of Ahura-Mazda and of Mithra in equally
conspicuous positions on the sculptured tablet above
his tomb ; and his example was followed by all
the later monarchs of his race whose sepulchres are
still in existence.[3] Artaxerxes Mnemon placed an
image of Mithra in the temple attached to the royal
palace at Susa.[4] He also in his inscriptions unites
Mithra with Ahura-Mazda, and prays for their con-
joint protection.[5] Artaxerxes Ochus does the same
a little later ;[6] and the practice is also observed in

[1] "Zendavesta," iii. 72 (Spiegel's edition).

[2] Haug, "Essays," p. 231.

[3] See the Author's "Ancient Monarchies," vol. iv. p. 334, and
Flandin, "Voyage en Perse," pls. 164 bis, 166, 173–176.

[4] Loftus, "Chaldæa and Susiana," p. 372.

[5] *Ibid.*

[6] Sir H. Rawlinson "Cuneiform Inscriptions," vol. i. p. 342.

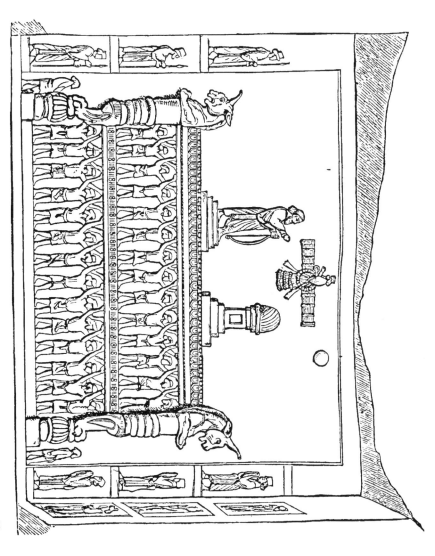

TOMB OF DARIUS.

89

portions of the Zendavesta composed about this period.[1] Ahura-Mazda and Mithra are called " the two
great ones," " the two great, imperishable, and pure."[2]

The position of man in the cosmic scheme was
determined by the fact that he was among the crea-
tions of Ahura-Mazda. Formed and placed on earth
by the Good Being, he was bound to render him
implicit obedience, and to oppose to the utmost
Angro-Mainyus and his creatures. His duties might
be summed up under the four heads of piety, purity,
industry, and veracity. Piety was to be shown by
an acknowledgment of Ahura-Mazda as the One
True God, by a reverential regard for the Amesha-
Spentas and the Izeds, or lower angels, by the frequent offering of prayers, praises, and thanksgivings,
the recitation of hymns, the occasional sacrifice of
animals, and the performance from time to time of a
curious ceremony known as that of the Haoma or
Homa. This consisted in the extraction of the juice
of the Homa plant by the priests during the recitation of prayers, the formal presentation of the liquid
extracted to the sacrificial fire, the consumption of a
small portion of it by one of the officiating ministers,
and the division of the remainder among the worshippers.[3] In sacrifices the priests were also necessary
go-betweens. The most approved victim was the
horse;[4] but it was likewise allowable to offer oxen,

[1] "Yasna," i. 34; ii. 44; iii. 48; "Mihr Yasht," 113.
[2] See Pusey's " Lectures on Daniel," p. 542, note 3.
[3] See Haug, " Essays," p. 239.
[4] "Yasna," xliv. 18. Compare Xen. "Cyrop." viii. 3, § 24;
and Ovid, "Fasti," i. 385.

sheep, or goats. The animal having been brought before an altar on which burnt the sacred fire, kindled originally (according to the general belief) from heaven, was there slain by a priest, who took of the flesh and *showed* it to the sacrificial fire, after which the victim was cooked and eaten at a solemn meal by the priests and worshippers united.

The purity required of the Iranians was inward as well as outward. Outward purity had to be maintained by a multiplicity of external observances,[1] forming in their entirety a burden as heavy to bear as that imposed by the Mosaic ceremonial law on the people of Israel. But inward purity was not neglected. Not only were the Iranians required to refrain from all impure acts, but also from impure words, and even from impure thoughts. Ahura-Mazda was "the pure, the master of purity," and would not tolerate less than perfect purity in his votaries.

The industry required by the Zoroastrian religion was of a peculiar kind. Man was placed upon the earth to preserve Ahura-Mazda's "good creation;" and this could only be done by careful tilling of the soil, eradication of thorns and weeds, and reclamation of the tracts over which Angro-Mainyus had spread the curse of barrenness. To cultivate the soil was thus a religious duty:[2] the whole community was required to be agricultural; and either as proprietor, as farmer, or as labouring man, each Zoroastrian was

1 "Vendidad," Farg. 8–11, and 16, 17.
2 "Yasna," xxxiii. 3.

bound to "further the works of life" by advancing tillage.

The duty of veracity was inculcated perhaps more strenuously than any other. "The Persian youth are taught," says Herodotus,[1] "three things, and three things only: to ride, to draw the bow, and to speak the truth." Ahura-Mazda was the "*true spirit*,"[2] and the chief of the Amesha-Spentas was Asha-vahista, "the best *truth*." Druj, "falsehood," is held up to detestation, alike in the Zendavesta and in the Persian cuneiform inscriptions,[3] as the basest, the most contemptible, and the most pernicious of vices.

If it be asked what opinions were entertained by the Zoroastrians concerning man's ultimate destiny, the answer would seem to be, that they were devout and earnest believers in the immortality of the soul, and a conscious future existence. It was taught that immediately after death the souls of men, both good and bad, proceeded together along an appointed path to the "bridge of the gatherer." There was a narrow road conducting to heaven, or paradise, over which the souls of the good alone could pass, while the wicked fell from it into the gulf below, where they found themselves in the place of punishment. The pious soul was assisted across the bridge by the angel Serosh, "the happy, well-formed, swift, tall

[1] Herod. i. 136.

[2] "Yasna," xxxv. 3.

[3] Sir H. Rawlinson, "Cuneiform Inscriptions," vol. i. pp. 200, 244, 245, etc.

Serosh," who went out to meet the weary wayfarer, and sustained his steps as he effected the difficult passage. The prayers of his friends in this world much availed the deceased, and helped him forward greatly on his journey. As he entered the angel Vohu-mano rose from his throne, and greeted him with the words—"How happy art thou, who hast come here to us, exchanging mortality for immortality!" Then the good soul went joyfully onward to the golden throne, to paradise. As for the wicked, when they fell into the gulf, they found themselves in outer darkness, in the kingdom of Angro-Mainyus, where they were forced to remain in a sad and wretched condition.[1]

It has been maintained by some that the early Iranians also held the doctrine of the resurrection of the body.[2] Such a doctrine is certainly contained in the more recent portions of the Zendavesta; and it is argued that there are expressions in the more ancient parts of that work which imply it, if they do not actually assert it. But a careful examination of the passages adduced makes it evident, that no more is in reality asserted in them than the continued existence of the soul; and Spiegel comes to the conclusion that, even so late as the time when the "Vendidad" was written, "the resurrection of the body was not yet known to the Parsees,"[3] or Persians.

The original religion of the Iranians was Dualism

[1] "Vendidad," xix. 30–32; Haug, "Essays," p. 156.
[2] Haug, "Essays," p. 266.
[3] Spiegel, "Avesta," vol. ii. p. 248, 249.

of a very pronounced type, assigning, as it did, to
Angro-Mainyus complete independence of Ahura-
Mazda, and equal eternity with him, with almost
equal power. It verged upon polytheism by the
very important position which it assigned to certain
of the ahuras or angels, whom it coupled with the
Principle of Good in a way which derogated from
his supreme and unrivalled dignity.[1] In its morality
it maintained a high tone; but it imposed on its
followers a burdensome yoke of ceremonial observances. It taught a future life, with happiness for
the good and misery for the wicked; but unfortu-
nately inclined to identify goodness with orthodoxy,
and wickedness with a rejection of the doctrine of
Zoroaster.

It may help the reader to understand the inner
spirit of the religion, if we give one or two specimens
of the hymns which constituted so important a part
of the Zoroastrian worship. The following is one
of the Gâthas, and is by some assigned to Zoroaster
himself[2]:—

"Now will I speak and proclaim to all who have come to listen
Thy praise, Ahura-Mazda, and thine, O Vohu-mano.
Asha! I ask that thy grace may appear in the lights of heaven.

Hear with your ears what is best, perceive with your minds what
    is purest,

---

[1] Pusey, "Lectures on Daniel," p. 535, note 9.

[2] Hübschmann, "Ein Zoroastrisches Lie d, mit Rücksicht auf
die Tradition, übersetzt und erklart." München, 1872. Compare Max Müller, "Lectures on the Science of Religion," pp.
237–239.

So that each man for himself may, before the great doom cometh,
Choose the creed he prefers. May the wise ones be on our side.

These two Spirits are twins; they made known in times that are
     bygone
That which is good and evil, in thought, and word, and action.
Rightly decided between them the good; not so the evil.

When these Two came together, first of all they created
Life and death, that at last there might be for such as are evil
Wretchedness, but for the good a happy blest existence.

Of these Two the One who was evil chose what was evil;
He who was kind and good, whose robe was the changeless
     Heaven,
Chose what was right; those, too, whose works pleased Ahura-
     Mazda.

They could not rightly discern who erred and worshipped the
     Devas;
They the Bad Spirit chose, and, having held counsel together,
Turned to Rapine, that so they might make man's life an affliction.

But to the good came might; and with might came wisdom and
     virtue;
Armaiti herself, the Eternal, gave to their bodies
Vigour; e'en thou wert enriched by the gifts that she scatttered,
     O Mazda.

Mazda, the time will come when the crimes of the bad shall be
     punished;
Then shall thy power be displayed in fitly rewarding the right-
     eous—
Them that have bound and delivered up falsehood to Asha the
     Truth-God.

Let us then be of those who advance this world and improve it,
O Ahura-Mazda, O Truth-God bliss conferring!
Let our minds be ever there where wisdom abideth!

Then indeed shall be seen the fall of pernicious falsehood;
But in the house where dwell Vohu-mano, Mazda, and Asha—
Beautiful house—shall be gathered for ever such as are worthy.

O men, if you but cling to the precepts Mazda has given,
Precepts, which to the bad are a torment, but joy to the righteous,
Then shall you one day find yourselves victorious through them."

Our other specimen is taken from the " Yasna," or " Book on Sacrifice," and is probably some centuries later than the great bulk of the Gathas[1] :—

"We worship Ahura-Mazda, the pure, the master of purity:
We worship the Amesha-Spentas, possessors and givers of blessings:

We worship the whole creation of Him who is True, the heavenly,
With the terrestrial, all that supports the good creation,
All that favours the spread of the good Mazd-yasna[2] religion.

We praise whatever is good in thought, in word, or in action,
Past or future; we also keep clean whatever is excellent.

O Ahura-mazda, thou true and happy being!
We strive both to think, and to speak, and to do whatever is fittest
Both our lives[3] to preserve, and bring them both to perfection.

Holy Spirit of Earth, for our best works'[4] sake, we entreat thee,
Grant us beautiful fertile fields—aye, grant them to all men,
Believers and unbelievers, the wealthy and those that have
   nothing."

---

[1] Haug, "Essays," pp. 162, 163.

[2] "Mazd-yasna" means "Ahura-mazda worshipping." *Mazdisn* was used commonly to designate the orthodox, under the Sassa-nians.

[3] The two lives are "the life of the soul" and "the life of the body" (Haug, "Essays," l. s. c.).

[4] *i. e.* "our agricultural labours" (*ibid.*).

The religion of the early Iranians became corrupted after a time by an admixture of foreign superstitions. The followers of Zoroaster, as they spread themselves from their original seat upon the Oxus over the regions lying south and south-west of the Caspian Sea, were brought into contact with a form of faith considerably different from that to which they had previously been attached, yet well adapted for blend-

FIRE ALTARS.

ing with it. This was Magism, or the worship of the elements. The early inhabitants of Armenia, Cappadocia, and the Zagros mountain-range, had, under circumstances that are unknown to us, developed this form of religion, and had associated with its tenets a priest-caste, claiming prophetic powers,

and a highly sacerdotal character. The essentials of
the religion were these : the four elements, fire, air,
earth, and water, were recognised as the only proper
objects of human reverence. Personal gods, and
together with them temples, shrines, and images,
were rejected. The devotion of the worshippers was
paid, not to any powers presiding over the constituent
parts of nature, but to those constituent parts themselves. Fire, as the most subtle and ethereal principle, and again as the most powerful agent, attracted
especial regard ; and on the fire-altars of the Magians
the sacred flame, generally regarded as kindled from
heaven, was kept uninterruptedly burning from year
to year, and from age to age, by bands of priests,
whose special duty it was to see that the sacred spark
was never extinguished. To defile the altar by
blowing the flame with one's breath was a capital
offence, and to burn a corpse was regarded as equally
odious. When victims were offered, nothing but a
small portion of the fat was consumed in the flames.
Next to fire, water was reverenced. Sacrifice was
offered to rivers, lakes, and fountains, the victim
being brought near to them and then slain, while
the utmost care was taken that no drop of their
blood should touch the water and pollute it. No
refuse was allowed to be cast into a river, nor was
it even lawful to wash one's hands in one. Reverence for earth was shown by sacrifice and by absten-
tion from the usual mode of burying the dead.[1]

---

[1] The chief authorities for this description are Herodotus (i.
132), Strabo (xv. 3, §§ 13, 14), and Agathias (ii. 24).

The Magian priest-caste held an exalted position. No worshipper could perform any rite of the religion unless by the intervention of a priest, who stood between him and the Deity as a mediator.[1] The Magus prepared the victim and slew it, chanted the mystic strain which gave the sacrifice all its force, poured on the ground the propitiatory libation of oil, milk, and honey, and held the bundle of thin tamarisk twigs, the barsom (*baresma*) of the later Zend books, the employment of which was essential to every sacrificial ceremony.[2] Claiming supernatural powers, they explained omens, expounded dreams, and by means of a certain mysterious manipulation of the barsom, or bundle of tamarisk-twigs,[3] arrived at a knowledge of future events, which they would sometimes condescend to communicate to the pious inquirer.

With such pretensions it was natural that the caste should assume a lofty air, a stately dress, and an environment of ceremonial magnificence. Clad in white robes, and bearing upon their heads tall felt caps, with long lappets at the sides, which (we are told[4]) concealed the jaw and even the lips, each with his barsom in his hand, they marched in procession to the fire-altars, and standing round them performed for an hour at a time their magical incantations. The credulous multitude, impressed by sights of this kind,

---

[1] Herod. l. s. c.; Amm. Marc. **xxiii**. 6.

[2] Strabo, l. s. c.

[3] Dino, Fr. 8; Schol. ad. Nic. Ther. 613.

[4] Strabo, **xv**. 3, § 15; Diog. Laert. "Procm."

and imposed on by the claims to supernatural powers which the Magi put forward, paid them a willing homage; the kings and chiefs consulted them; and

MAGIAN PRIEST.

when the Iranians, pressing westward, came into contact with the races professing the Magian religion, they found the Magian priest-caste all-powerful in most of the western nations.

Originally Zoroastrianism had been intolerant and

exclusive. Its first professors had looked with aversion and contempt on the creed of their Indian brethren; they had been fierce opponents of idolatry, and absolutely hostile to every form of religion except that which they had themselves worked out. But with the lapse of time these feelings had grown weaker. The old religious fervour had abated. An impressible and imitative spirit had developed itself. When the Zoroastrians came into contact with Magism, it impressed them favourably. There was no contradiction between its main tenets and those of their old religion; they were compatible, and might readily be held together; and the result was, that, without giving up any part of their previous creed, the Iranians adopted and added on to it all the principal points of the Magian belief, and all the more remarkable of the Magian religious usages. This religious fusion seems first to have taken place in Media. The Magi became a Median tribe,[1] and were adopted as the priest-caste of the Median nation. Elemental worship, divination by means of the barsom, dream-expounding, incantations at the fire-altars, sacrifices whereat a Magus officiated, were added on to the old dualism and qualified worship of the Amesha-Spentas, of Mithra, and of the other ahuras; and a mixed or mongrel religion was thus formed, which long struggled with, and ultimately prevailed over, pure Zoroastrianism.[2] The Persians

[1] Herod. i. 101.

[2] See Westergaard's "Introduction to the Zendavesta," p. 17; and compare the Author's "Essay on the Religion of the Ancient Persians" in his "Herodotus," vol. i. pp. 414–419, 3rd edition.

after a time came into this belief, accepted the Magi for their priests, and attended the ceremonies at the fire-altars.

The adoption of elemental worship into the Iranian system produced a curious practice with regard to dead bodies. It became unlawful to burn them, since that would be a pollution of fire; or to bury them, thereby polluting earth; or to throw them into a river, thereby polluting water; or even to place them in a sepulchral chamber, or a sarcophagus, since that would cause a pollution of air. What, then, was to be done with them? In what way were they to be disposed of? Some races of men, probably moved by these scruples, adopted the practice, which they regarded as eminently pious, of killing those who, they suspected, were about to die, and then eating them.[1] But the Iranians had reached that stage of civilisation when cannibalism is held to be disgusting. Disinclined to devour their dead themselves, they hit on an expedient which, without requiring them to do what they so much disliked, had the same result—transferred, that is, the bodies of their departed friends into those of other living organisms, and so avoided the pollution of any element by their decaying remains. Immediately after death they removed the bodies to a solitary place, and left them to be devoured by beasts and birds of prey, crows, ravens, vultures, wolves, jackals, and foxes. This was the orthodox practice,[2] was employed by

---

[1] Herod. i. 216; iii. 99.

[2] Strabo, xv. 3, § 20.   Compare Herod. i. 140.

the Magi themselves in the case of their own dead, and was earnestly recommended to others;[1] but as it was found that, despite all exhortations, there were some whose prejudices would not allow them to adopt this method, another had to be devised and allowed, though not recommended. This was the coating of the dead body with wax previously to its deposition in the ground.[2] Direct contact between the corpse and the earth being in this way prevented, pollution was supposed to be avoided.

The mixed religion thus constituted, though less elevated and less pure than the original Zoroastrian creed, must be pronounced to have possessed a certain loftiness and picturesqueness which suited it to become the religion of a great and splendid monarchy. The mysterious fire-altars upon the mountain-tops, with their prestige of a remote antiquity—the ever-burning flame believed to have been kindled from on high—the worship in the open air under the blue canopy of heaven—the long troops of Magians in their white robes, with their strange caps, and their mystic wands—the frequent prayers, the abundant sacrifices, the low incantations—the supposed prophetic powers of the priest-caste—all this together constituted an imposing whole at once to the eye and to the mind, and was calculated to give additional grandeur to the civil system that should be allied with it. Pure Zoroastrianism was too spiritual to coalesce readily with Oriental luxury and magnifi-

---

[1] "Vendidad," Farg. v. to viii.

[2] Herod. l. s. c.; Strabo, l. s. c.

cence, or to lend strength to a government based on the principles of Asiatic despotism. Magism furnished a hierarchy to support the throne and add splendour and dignity to the court while it overawed the subject class by its supposed possession of supernatural powers and of the right of mediating between man and God. It supplied a picturesque worship, which at once gratified the senses and excited the fancy. It gave scope to man's passion for the marvellous by its incantations, its divining-rods, its omen-reading, and its dream-expounding. It gratified the religious scrupulosity which finds a pleasure in making to itself difficulties, by the disallowance of a thousand natural acts, and the imposition of numberless rules for external purity. At the same time it gave no offence to the anti-idolatrous spirit in which the Iranians had always gloried, but upheld and encouraged the iconoclasm which they had previously practised. It thus blended easily with the previous creed of the Iranian people, and produced an amalgam that has shown a surprising vitality, having lasted above two thousand years—from the time of Xerxes, the son of Darius Hystaspis (B. C. 485–465) to the present day.

CHAPTER IV.

THE RELIGION OF THE EARLY SANSKRITIC INDIANS.

"Le panthéisme naturaliste et le polytheisme, sa conséquence inévitable, s'etaient graduellement introduits dans les croyances des Aryas."–LENORMANT, *Manuel d' Histoire Ancienne*, vol. iii. p. 309.

THE religion of the early Indians, like that of the Egyptians, and like that of Assyrians and Babylonians, was an extensive polytheism, but a polytheism of a very peculiar character. There lay behind it, at its first formation, no conscious monotheism, no conception of a single supreme power, from whom man and nature, and all the forces in nature, have their origin. If we hold, as I believe we do right to hold, that God revealed Himself to the first parents of the human race as a single personal being, and so that all races of men had at the first this idea as an inheritance handed down to them traditionally from their ancestors, yet it would seem certain that in India, before the religion which we find in the Vedas arose, this belief had completely faded away and disappeared ; the notion of "God" had passed into the notion of "gods;" a real polytheism universally prevailed, even with the highest

class of intellects ;[1] and when, in the course of time,
monotheistic ideas showed themselves, they sprang
up in individual minds as the results of individual
speculation,[2] and were uttered tentatively, not as doctrines, but as hypotheses, as timid " guesses at truth,"
on the part of those who confessed that they knew
little or nothing.

If it be asked how this forgetfulness came about,
how the idea of one God, once possessed, could ever
be lost, perhaps we may find an answer in that fact to
which the traditions of the race and some of their
peculiar expressions[3] point back, that for many centuries they had been located in one of the cruellest
regions of the earth, a region with " ten months of
winter and two months of summer,"[4] where the
struggle for existence must have been terrible indeed,
and all their energies, all their time, all their thought,
must have been spent on the satisfaction of those
physical needs for which provision must be made before man can occupy himself with the riddle of the
universe.   At any rate, however we may account for
it, or whether we can account for it or no, the fact
remains ; somehow or other the Sanskritic Indians
had ceased to " retain God in their knowledge ;"[5]

[1] See Max Müller, "Ancient Sanskrit Literature," pp. 528, 529.
[2] *Ibid.* p. 559.
[3] As the expression, "a hundred *winters*," used for a hundred
years. (See H. H. Wilson's "Introduction to the Rig-Veda,"
vol. i. p. xlii.)
[4] See the description of "Aryanem vaejo"—the old home of
the Aryans—in the First Fargard of the "Vendidad" ("Ancient
Monarchies," vol. ii. p. 432).
[5] Romans i. 28.

they were for a time "without God in the world," they had lost the sense of His " eternal power and Godhead ;"[1] they were in the condition that men would be in who should be veritable "children of the soil," springing into life without inheritance of ancestral notions.

But there was one thing which they could not be without. God has implanted in all men a religious faculty, a religious instinct, which is an essential portion of their nature and among the faculties which most distinguish man from the brutes. No sooner was the tension produced by the severe character of their surroundings relaxed—no sooner did the plains of the Punjab receive the previous dwellers in the Hindu Kush—than this instinct asserted itself, perceived that there was something divine in the world, and proceeded to the manufacture of deities. Nature seemed to the Hindoo not to be one, but many ; and all nature seemed to be wonderful and, so, divine. The sky, the air, the dawn, the sun, the earth, the moon, the wind, the storms, fire, the waters, the rivers, attracted his attention, charmed him, sometimes terrified him, seemed to him instinct with power and life, became to him objects of admiration and then of worship. At first, it would appear, the objects themselves were adored ; but the objects received names ; the names were, by the laws of Indian grammar, masculine or feminine ; and the named objects thus passed into persons,[2] the *nomina* became

[1] Romans i. 20.

[2] Max Müller, " Lectures on the Science of Religion," pp. 54–56.

numina, beings quite distinct from the objects themselves, presiding over them, directing them, ruling them, but having a separate and another kind of existence.

And now the polytheism, already sufficiently extensive through the multiplicity of things natural, took a fresh start. The names, having become persons, tended to float away from the objects; and the objects received fresh names, which in their turn were exalted into gods, and so swelled the pantheon. When first the idea of counting the gods presented itself to the mind of a Vedic poet, and he subjected them to a formal census, he found them to amount to no more than thirty-three.[1] But in course of time this small band swelled into a multitude, and Visvamitra, a somewhat late poet, states the number at 3,339.[2]

One of the features most clearly pronounced in the Vedic polytheism is that which has been already noticed as obtaining to a considerable extent both in the Egyptian and Assyrian religions,[3] the feature which has been called " Kathenotheism " or " Henotheism."[4] A Vedic worshipper, for the most part, when he turned his regards towards any individual deity, forgot for the time being that there was any other, and addressed the immediate object of his

---

[1] Rig-Veda, viii. 30. (See Max Müller s "Ancient Sanskrit Literature," p. 531.)

[2] "Rig-Veda Sanhita" (translation of H. H. Wilson), vol. iii. p. 7.

[3] See above, pp. 40 and 56.

[4] Max Muller, "Chips from a German Workshop," vol. i. p. 28; "Science of Religion," p. 141.

adoration in terms of as absolute devotion as if he were the sole God whom he recognised, the one and only Divine Being in the entire universe. " In the first hymn of the second Mandala, the god Agni is called ' the ruler of the universe,' ' the lord of men,' ' the wise king, the father, the brother, the son, the friend of man ; ' nay, all the powers and names of the other gods are distinctly assigned to Agni."[1] Similarly, in another hymn, Varuna is " ' the wise god,' the ' lord of all,' ' the lord of heaven and earth,' ' the upholder of order,' ' he who gives to men glory.'[2] It is the same with Indra—he is ' the ruler of all that moves,' the ' mighty one,' ' he to whom there is none like in heaven or earth : ' "[3] " the gods," it is said, " do not reach thee, Indra, nor men ; thou overcomest all creatures in strength." The best authority tells us that " it would be easy to find, in the numerous hymns of the Veda, passages in which almost every important deity is represented as supreme and absolute."[4] At the same time there is no rivalry, no comparison of one god with another, no conflict of opinion between the votaries of different deities ; each is supreme and absolute in his turn, simply because " all the rest disappear for a moment from the vision of the poet, and he only who is to fulfil their desires stands in full light before the eyes of the worshippers."[5]

[1] "Chips," l. s. c.
[2] " Ancient Sanskrit Literature," pp. 536, 537.
[3] *Ibid.* p. 546.
[4] "Chips from a German Workshop," p. 28.
[5] *Ibid.*

Among the various deities thus, in a certain sense, equalised, there are three who may be said to occupy, if not the chief, at any rate the oldest place, since their names have passed out of the sphere of mere appellatives, and have become proper names, the designations of distinct persons. These are Varuna, Mitra, and Indra—originally, the Sky, the Sun, and the Storm (or, perhaps, the Day)—but, in the Vedic hymns, only slightly connected with any particular aspects of nature, and not marked off by any strong differences the one from the other. Indra, indeed, is the main object of adoration ; more than one-third of the hymns in the earlier part of the Rig-Veda are addressed to him.[1] He is " the sovereign of the world," " the all-wise," " the abode of truth," " the lord of the good," " the animator of all," " the show-erer of benefits," " the fulfiller of the desire of him who offers praise ;"[2] and, with more or less of refer-ence to his original character, " the sender of rain," " the giver of food," " the lord of opulence," and " the wielder of the thunderbolt."[3]   Varuna is more sparingly addressed ; but, when addressed, is put quite upon a par with Indra, joined with him in such phrases as " sovereign Indra and Varuna," " Indra and Varuna, sovereign rulers," " divine Indra and

[1] Forty-five in the first Astaka, out of 121; 39 in the second, out of 118; 48 in the third, out of 121 ; and 46 in fourth, out of 140—altogether 178 out of 502. (See the "Introduction" of Prof. H. H. Wilson to his "Translation of the Rig-Veda Sanhita.")

[2] Rig-Veda, vol. ii. pp. 36, 145, 283; vol. iii. pp. 157, 159, and 166.

[3] *Ibid.* vol. ii. p. 283; vol. iii. pp. 157 and 160.

Varuna," "mighty Indra and Varuna,"[1] etc., and entreated to afford the worshipper, equally with Indra, protection, long life, riches, sons and grandsons, happiness. Mitra is the usual companion of Varuna, sharing with him in the fifth Mandala eleven consecutive hymns,[2] and elsewhere joined with him frequently;[3] they are "observers of truth," "imperial rulers of the world," "lords of heaven and truth," "protectors of the universe," "mighty deities," "far-seeing," "excelling in radiance;"[4] they "uphold the three realms of light," "scatter foes," "guide men in the right way," "send rain from heaven," "grant men their desires,"[5] "procure for them exceeding and perfect felicity."[6] They ride together in one chariot, which "shines in the firmament like lightning;"[7] they sustain the sun in his course, and conjointly cause the rain to fall; they are "possessed of irresistible strength,"[8] and uphold the celestial and terrestrial worlds."[9] It can scarcely be doubted that Mitra was once the sun, as Mithra always was in Persia;[10] but in the hymns of the Rig-Veda he has passed out of that subordinate position, and has

---

[1] "Rig-Veda," vol. i. p. 40; vol. iii. pp. 63, 201, 203, etc.

[2] *Ibid.* vol. iii. pp. 347–357.

[3] As in vol. i. pp. 7, 117, and 230; vol. ii. pp. 3–6, 53–55, 59, etc.

[4] Wilson's "Introduction," vol. iii. pp. 349–354.

[5] Wilson's "Introduction," vol. iii. pp. 354–356.

[6] *Ibid.* p. 349. [7] *Ibid.* p. 348.

[8] *Ibid.* pp. 353, 354.

[9] *Ibid.* p. 356.

[10] See the Author's "Ancient Monarchies," vol. ii. p. 328; vol. iii. pp. 348 and 352.

become a god who sustains the sun, and who has a general power over the elements. His place as the actual sun-god has been taken by another and distinct deity, of whom more will be said presently.

Next to these three gods, whose character is rather general than special, must be placed Agni—the Latin *ignis*—who is distinctly the god of fire. Fire presented itself to the early Indians under a twofold aspect;[1] first, as it exists on earth, on the hearth, on the altar, and in the conflagration; secondly, as it exists in the sky, in the shape of lightning, meteors, stars, comets, and light generally, so far as that is independent of the sun. The earthly aspect of fire is most dwelt upon. The Vedic poet sees it leaping forth from darkness on the rapid friction of two sticks in the hands of a strong man. It is greedy for food as it steps forth out of its prison, it snorts like a horse as with loud crackle it seizes and spreads among the fuel. Then for a moment its path is darkened by great folds of smoke; but it overcomes, it triumphs, and mounts up in a brilliant column of pure clear flame into the sky.[2] As culinary fire, Agni is the supporter of life, the giver of strength and vigour, the imparter of a pleasant flavour to food,[3] the diffuser of happiness in a dwelling. As sacrificial fire, he is the messenger between the other

[1] Wilson says "a three-fold aspect" ("Introduction to Rig-Veda," vol. i. p. xxvii), distinguishing between the region of the air and that of the sky; but the Vedic poets scarcely make this distinction.

[2] See Max Müller, "Ancient Sanskrit Literature," p.547, note.

[3] Rig-Veda, vol. iii. pp. 184, 247, etc.

gods and man; the interpreter to the other gods of human wants; the all-wise, who knows every thought of the worshipper; the bestower of all blessings on men, since it is by his intervention alone that their offerings are conveyed, and their wishes made known to any deity. As conflagration, Agni is "the consumer of forests, the dark-pathed, the bright-shining."[1] "White-hued, vociferous, abiding in the firmament with the imperishable resounding winds, the youngest of the gods, Agni, purifying and most vast, proceeds, feeding upon numerous and substantial forests. His bright flames, fanned by the wind, spread wide in every direction, consuming abundant fuel; divine, fresh-rising, they play upon the woods, enveloping them in lustre."[2] Occasionally, instead of consuming forests, he devours cities with their inhabitants. When the Aryan Indians prevail over their enemies and give their dwellings to the flames, it is Agni who "destroys the ancient towns of the dispersed,"[3] and "consumes victorious all the cities of the foe and their precious things."[4] Hence, he is constantly invoked against enemies, and exhorted to overthrow them, to give their cities to destruction, to "burn them down like pieces of dry timber,"[5] to chastise them and "consume them entirely." In his celestial character, Agni, on the other hand, is, comparatively speaking, but rarely recognized. Still,

[1] Rig-Veda, p. 391.
[2] *Ibid.* vol. iii. Compare pp. 136, 254, 385, etc.
[3] *Ibid.* p. 388.
[4] *Ibid.* p. 16.   [5] *Ibid.* p. 126.

his frequent association with Indra[1] points to this
aspect of him. Both he and Indra are " wielders of
the thunderbolt ;"[2] they occupy a common car;[3]
they are joint " slayers of Vitra ;"[4] and Agni is described in once place as " the agitator of the
clouds when the rain is poured forth," he who,
" moving with the swiftness of the wind, shines with
a pure radiance ; " whose " falling rays, accompanied
by the moving storms, strike against the cloud,"
which thereupon " roars," after which " the shower
comes with delightful and smiling drops, the rain
descends, the clouds thunder." [5]

After Agni we may place in a single group, Dyaus,
" the heaven ;" Surya, or Savitri, "the sun ;" Soma,
" the moon ;" Ushas, " the dawn ;" Prithivi, " the
earth ;" Vayu, " the wind ;" Ap, " the waters ;" Nadi,
" the rivers ;" and the Maruts, " the storms." These
are all nature-gods of a very plain and simple kind,
corresponding to the Greek Uranus, Heelios, Selene,
Eos, Ge, or Gaia, etc., and to the Roman Cœlus,
Apollo. Luna, Aurora, Tellus, Æolus, etc. Of all
these the Maruts are the most favourite objects of worship, having twenty-four hymns devoted to them in
the first six Mandalas of the Rig-Veda.[6] Next to

---

[1] Mandala i. 21, 108; Mandala iii. 12; Mandala v. 14; Mandala vi. 59; etc.

[2] Rig-Veda, vol. iii. p. 500.

[3] *Ibid.* p. 501.

[4] *Ibid.* vol. iii. pp. 111, 503, etc.

[5] *Ibid.* vol. i. p. 202.

[6] See Wilson's "Introductions" to the several volumes of the
Rig-Veda Sanhita, vol. i. p. 15; vol. iii. p. 7.

these may be placed Ushas, who has eleven hymns; then Dyaus and Prithivi, who share seven hymns; after these Surya, who has six; then Vayu, who has two; then Soma, who has one; and lastly, Ap and Nadi, who are not worshipped separately at all. Ushas, the dawn, is perhaps the most beautiful creation of the Vedic bards. "She is the friend of men; she smiles like a young wife; she is the daughter of the sky. She goes to every house; she thinks of the dwellings of men; she does not despise the small or the great; she brings wealth; she is always the same, immortal, divine; age cannot touch her; she is the young goddess, but she makes men grow old."[1] Born again and again, and with bright unchanging hues, she dissipates the accumulated glooms, anoints her beauty as the priests anoint the sacrificial food in sacrifices, bright-shining she smiles, like a flatterer, to obtain favour, then lights up the world, spreads, expanding westward with her radiance, awakes men to consciousness, calls forth the pleasant sounds of bird and beast, arouses all things that have life to their several labours.[2] Sometimes a mere natural appearance, more often a manifest goddess, she comes before men day after day with ever young and fresh beauty, challenging their admiration, almost forcing them to worship her. The lazy inhabitants of so-called civilised lands, who rarely leave their beds till the sun has been up for hours, can scarcely understand the sentiments with which a simple race, that went to rest

---

[1] Max Müller, "Ancient Sanskrit Literature," p. 551.
[2] Rig-Veda, vol. i. pp. 236–238 and 298, 299.

with the evening twilight, awaited each morning the coming of the rosy-fingered dawn, or the ecstatic joy with which they saw the darkness in the eastern sky fade and lift before the soft approach of something tenderer and lovelier than day.

Surya, " the sun," does not play a prominent part in the Vedic poems.[1] Out of the five hundred hymns in Wilson's collection, only six are devoted to him exclusively.[2] His presentation is nearly that of Heelios in the Greek, and Phœbus Apollo in the Roman mythology. Brilliant, many-rayed, adorable, he yokes each morning his two,[3] or seven,[4] swift coursers to his car, and mounts up the steep incline of heaven, following Ushas, as a youth pursues a maiden, and destroying her.[5] Journeying onward at incredible speed [6] between the two regions

[1] Wilson, "Introduction to Rig-Veda," vol. i. p. xxxii.

[2] Mandala i. Suktas 50 and 115; Mandala ii. Sukta 38; and Mandala v. Suktas 81 and 82. Surya has also a part in Mandala i. Sukta 35; Mandala v. Suktas 40 and 45; and Mandala vi. Sukta 50.

[3] Rig-Veda, vol. i. p. 98.

[4] *Ibid.* p. 133.

[5] *Ibid.* p. 304. Compare Max Müller's "Ancient Sanskrit Literature," pp. 529, 530, where the following comment of an Indian critic is quoted:—"It is fabled that Prajapati, the Lord of Creation, did violence to his daughter. But what does it mean? Prajapati, the Lord of Creation, is a name of the sun; and he is called so because he protects all creatures. His daughter, Ushas, is the Dawn. And when it is said that he was in love with her, this only means that, at sunrise, the sun runs after the dawn, the dawn being at the same time called the daughter of the sun, because she rises when he approaches."

[6] *Ibid.* vol. i. p. 132.

of heaven and earth, he pours down his quickening, life-bestowing, purifying rays on all, dispels diseases,[1] gives fertility, and multiplies wealth.[2] Having attained the summit of the sky, he commences his descent, and travelling on a downward path, conducts his car with safety to the far limits of the west, carrying off with him all the diffused rays of light,[3] and disappearing, no one knows whither.[4]

Vayu, the " wind," generally coupled with Indra, as a god of heaven, has only two whole hymns,[5] and parts of five others, devoted to him in Wilson's collection. What is chiefly celebrated is his swiftness; and in this connection he has sometimes ninety-nine, sometimes a hundred,[6] sometimes a thousand steeds,[7] or even a thousand chariots,[8] assigned to him. The colour of his horses is red or purple.[9] He is "swift as thought," he has "a thousand eyes," and is "the protector of pious acts."[10] As one of the gods who "sends rain,"[11] he is invoked frequently by the inhabitants of a country where want of rain is equivalent to a famine.

Dyaus and Prithivi, "heaven" and "earth," are

[1] Rig-Veda, vol. i. pp. 99 and 134.
[2] *Ibid.* vol. ii. pp. 307, 309, etc.
[3] *Ibid.* vol. i. p. 305.
[4] *Ibid.* p. 99.
[5] Mandala ii. Sukta 134; and Mandala vi. Sukta 48.
[6] Rig-Veda, vol. iii. p. 211.
[7] *Ibid.* pp. 210 and 212. Compare vol. ii. p. 49.
[8] *Ibid.* vol. ii. p. 313.
[9] *Ibid.* p. 46.
[10] *Ibid.* vol. i. p. 55.
[11] *Ibid.* vol. iii. p. 487.

mostly coupled together, and addressed in the same hymns; but, besides the joint addresses, Prithivi is sometimes the sole subject of a sacred poem.[1] Dyaus has occasionally the epithet of *pitar*, or " father,"[2] and thus, so far as the name goes, undoubtedly corresponds with the Jupiter or Diespiter of the Romans. But he is certainly not in the same way the " father," or creator, of the other gods. Rather, some individual poets, in their craving after divine sympathy and communion, have ventured to bestow on him the name of " father " exceptionally, not with any intention of making him the head of the Pantheon, but as claiming to themselves a share in the Divine nature, and expressing the same feeling as the Greek poet when he said, " For we are also his offspring."[3]

It is unnecessary to detain the reader with a complete account of the rest of the thirty-three gods. Some, as Aditi, Pushan, Brahmaspati, Brihaspati, Panjaniya, seem to be mere duplicate or triplicate names of deities already mentioned. Others, as the Aswins, Aryaman, Rudra, Vishnu, Yama, belong to a lower grade, being rather demigods or heroes than actual deities. Others, again, are indistinct, and of little importance, as Saraswati, Bhaga, Twashtri, Parvata, Hotra, Bharati, Sadi, Varutri, and Dhishana.

Special attention must, however, be called to Soma. By a principle of combination which is quite inscrutable, Soma represents at once the moon or moon-

---

[1] Mandala v. Sukta 83.

[2] Max Müller, "Science of Religion," p. 172.

[3] Acts xvii. 28.   St. Paul, as is well known, quoted Aratus.

god, and the genius presiding over a certain plant. The assignment of a sacred character to the Soma, or Homa plant (*Sarcostema viminalis*),[1] was common to the Indic with the Iranian religion, though the use made of it in the two worships was different. According to the ordinary spirit of the Indic religion, a deity was required to preside over, or personify, this important part of nature, and the god chosen was the same that had the moon under his protection. Hence arises, in the hymns to Soma, a curious complication; and it is often difficult to determine which view of the god is present to the mind of the poet. The notion of the plant is the predominant one; but intermixed with it in the strangest way come touches which can only be explained by referring them to Soma's lunar character.[2]

The worship of their gods by the Indians was of a very simple kind, consisting of prayer, praise, and offerings. It was wholly domestic, that is to say, there were no temples or general places of assembly; but each man in his dwelling-house, in a chamber devoted to religious uses, performed, or rather had performed for him, the sacred rites which he preferred, and on which he placed his dependence for material and perhaps for spiritual blessings. An order of priests existed, by whom alone could religious services be conducted; and of these a goodly array officiated on all occasions, the number being

[1] H. H. Wilson, in notes to the Rig-Veda, vol. i. p. 6, note *a*.

[2] *Ibid.* p. 235, note *a*.

sometimes seven, at other times as many as sixteen.[1] It was not necessary for the worshipper to appear personally, or to take any part in the ceremony; enough was done if he provided the chamber, the altar, and the offerings. The chamber had to be spread with the *Kusa*, or sacred rushes; the fire had to be lighted upon the altar;[2] and then the worship commenced. Priests chanted in turn the verses of the *Mantras* or sacred hymns, which combined prayer with praise, and invited the presence of the deities. At the proper moment, when by certain mystic signs the priests knew the god or gods invoked to have arrived,[3] the offerings were presented, the divine favour secured, the prayers recited, and the ceremony brought to a close by some participation of the ministering priests in the offerings.

The praises, with which the hymns generally commence, describe the power, the wisdom, the grandeur, the marvellousness, the generosity, the goodness of the deity addressed, adding in some instances encomiums on his personal beauty[4] and the splendour of his dress and decorations.[5] Occasionally, his

---

[1] See Wilson's "Introduction" to vol. i. p. xxiv.

[2] It has been questioned whether the fire was not kept burning continually, as in the Persian Fire Temples (Wilson, "Introduction" to vol. i. of Rig-Veda, p. xxiii.); but the constant allusions to the production of fire by friction make it clear that, ordinarily, a fresh fire was kindled.

[3] Haug, "Essays on the Sacred Language, etc., of the Parsees," p. 248.

[4] Wilson, "Introduction," vol. i. p. xxiv. See also Mandala i. Sukta 9, § 3; Sukta 42 § 10; etc.

[5] Rig-Veda, vol. i. p. 223.

great actions are described, either in general terms, or with special reference to certain exploits ascribed to him in the mythology.[1] When he has been thus rendered favourable, and the offerings have been made in the customary way, the character of the hymn changes from praise to prayer, and the god is implored to bestow blessings on the person who has instituted the ceremony, and sometimes, but not so commonly, on the author or reciter of the prayer. It is noticeable that the blessings prayed for are, predominantly, of a temporal and personal description.[2] The worshipper asks for food, life, strength, health, posterity; for wealth, especially in cattle, horses, and cows; for happiness; for protection against enemies, for victory over them, and sometimes for their destruction, particularly where they are represented as heretics. Protection against evil spirits is also occasionally requested. There is, comparatively speaking, little demand for moral benefits, for discernment, or improvement of character, or forgiveness of sin, or repentance, or peace of mind, or strength, to resist temptation. The sense of guilt is slight.[3] It is only "in some few instances

[1] This is especially the case in hymns addressed to Indra. (Rig-Veda, vol. i. pp. 85–93, 136–139, etc.).

[2] Wilson, "Introduction" to vol. i. of Rig-Veda, p. xxv.; Max Müller, "Chips from a German Workshop," vol. i. p. 27.

[3] Wilson, l. s. c. Max Müller says, on the other hand, that "the consciousness of sin is a *prominent* feature in the religion of the Veda" ("Chips," vol. i. p. 41). He means, probably, a noticeable feature, not prominent in the sense of its occurring frequently.

that hatred of untruth and abhorrence of sin are
expressed, and a hope uttered that the latter may
be repented of or expiated."[1]   Still such expressions
do occur.   They are not wholly wanting, as they
are in the utterances of the ancient Egyptians.
" Deliver us this day, O gods, from heinous sin," is
the concluding petition of one Sukta.[2]   " May our
sin be repented of," is the burthen of another.[3]
" Absolve us from the sins of our fathers, and from
those which we have committed with our own
bodies," is the prayer of a third.[4]   " Varuna is mer-
ciful, even to him who has committed sin," is the
declaration of a fourth.[5]   Now and then we even
seem to have before us a broken-hearted penitent,
one who truly feels, like David or the Publican, the
depth to which he has fallen, and who, " out of the
depths,"[6] cries to God for forgiveness.   " Let me
not yet, O Varuna, enter into the house of clay,"
i. e. the grave, says a Vedic worshipper;[7] " have
mercy, almighty, have mercy.   If I go along trem-
bling, like a cloud driven by the wind, have mercy,
almighty, have mercy.   Through want of strength,
thou strong and bright god, have I gone wrong;
have mercy, almighty, have mercy.   Thirst came

---

[1] These are Prof. Wilson's words; and they are quite borne
out by the text of the Rig-Veda.

[2] Mandala i. Sukta 115, § 6.

[3] Mandala i. Sukta 97.

[4] Mandala vii. Sukta 86, § 5.

[5] Mandala vii. Sukta 87, § 7.

[6] Psa. cxxx. 1.

[7] Max Muller, ''Ancient Sanskrit Literature,'' p. 540.

upon the worshipper though he stood in the midst of the waters; have mercy, almighty, have mercy. Whenever we men, Varuna, commit an offence before the heavenly host, whenever we break the law through thoughtlessness; have mercy, almighty, have mercy."

The offerings wherewith the gods were propitiated were either victims or libations. Victims in the early times appear to have been but rarely sacrificed; and the only animals employed seem to have been the horse and the goat.[1] Libations were of three kinds: *ghee*, or clarified butter, honey,[2] and the expressed and fermented juice of the soma plant. The *ghee* and honey were poured upon the sacrificial fire; the soma juice was presented in ladles[3] to the deities invoked, part sprinkled on the fire, part on the *Kusa*, or sacred grass strewed upon the floor, and the rest in all cases drunk by those who had conducted the ceremony.[4] It is thought by some modern critics that the liquor offered to the gods was believed to intoxicate them, and that the priests took care to intoxicate themselves with the remainder;[5] but there is scarcely sufficient evidence for these charges. No doubt, the origin of the Soma ceremony must be referred to the exhilarating properties of the fermented

[1] On the sacrifice of these, see Rig-Veda, vol. ii. pp. 112–125.

[2] Honey is not common. On its use, see Max Muller, "Ancient Sanskrit Literature," pp. 535 and 537.

[3] Rig Veda, Mandala i. Sukta 116, § 24.

[4] Wilson, "Introduction" to vol. i. of Rig-Veda, p. xxiii.

[5] Haug? "Essays on the Sacred Language, etc., of the Parsees," pp. 247, 248.

juice, and to the delight and astonishment which
the discovery of them excited in simple minds.[1]
But exhilaration is a very different thing from
drunkenness; and, though Orientals do not often
draw the distinction, we are scarcely justified in
concluding, without better evidence than any which
has been adduced as yet, that the Soma ceremony
of the Hindoos was in the early ages a mere
Bacchanalian orgy, in which the worshippers in-
toxicated themselves in honour of approving deities.
Exhilaration will sufficiently explain all that is said
of the Soma in the Rig-Veda; and it is charitable
to suppose that nothing more was aimed at in the
Soma ceremony.

The offerings of praise and sacrifice, and especially
the offering of the soma juice, were considered not
merely to please the god, who was the object of them,
but to lay him under a binding obligation, and almost to compel him to grant the requests of the
worshipper. "The mortal who is strenuous in worship," it is said,[2] "acquires an authority" over the
object of his religious regards—an authority which
is so complete that he may even sell the god's favour
to another person, in order to enable him to attain
the object of his desires. "Who buys this—*my*
Indra," says Vamadeva, a Vedic poet,[3] "with ten
milch kine? When he shall have slain his foes,
then let the purchaser give him back to me again;"

[1] Wilson, "Introduction," p. xxxvii.
[2] Mandala iv. Sukta 15, § 5.
[3] *Ibid.* iv. Sukta 24, § 10.

which the commentator explains as follows:[1] "Vam-adeva, *having by much praise got Indra into his pos-session or subjugation*, proposes to make a bargain when about to dispose of him;" and so he offers for ten milch kine to hand him over temporarily, apparently to any person who will pay the price, with the proviso that when Indra has subdued the person's foes, he is to be returned to the vendor!

The subject of a future life seems scarcely to have presented itself with any distinctness to the thoughts of the early Indians. There is not the slightest appearance in the Rig-Veda of a belief in metempsychosis, or the transmigration of human souls after death into the bodies of animals.[2] The phenomena of the present world, what they see and hear and feel in it, in the rushing of the wind, the howling of the storm, the flashing of the lightning from cloud to cloud, the splash of the rain, the roar of the swollen rivers, the quick changes from day to night, and from night to day, from storm to calm and from calm to storm, from lurid gloom to sunshine and from sunshine to lurid gloom again; the interesting business of life, the kindling of fire, the lighting up of the hearth; the performance of sacrifice; the work, agricultural, pastoral, or other, to be done during the day, the storing up of food, the acquirement of riches, the training of children; war, the attack of foes, the crash of arms, the flight, the pursuit, the burning of towns, the carrying off of booty—these

---

[1] Wilson, Rig-Veda, vol. iii. p. 170, note 2.

[2] Max Müller, "Chips from a German Workshop," vol. i. p. 45.

things, and such things as these, so occupy and fill the minds of this primitive race, that they have in general no room for other speculations, no time or thought to devote to them. It is only occasionally, in rare instances, that to this or that poet the idea seems to have occurred, " Is this world the whole, or is there a hereafter? Are there such things as happiness and misery beyond the grave? Still, the Rig-Veda is not altogether without expressions which seem to indicate a hope of immortality and of future happiness to be enjoyed by the good, nor entirely devoid of phrases which may allude to a place of future punishment for the wicked. "He who gives alms," says one poet,[1] "goes to the highest place in heaven ; he goes to the gods." "Thou, Agni, hast announced heaven to Manu," says another; which is explained to mean, that Agni revealed to Manu the fact, that heaven is to be gained by pious works.[2] "Pious sacrificers," proclaims a third,[3] "enjoy a residence in the heaven of Indra; pious sacrificers dwell in the presence of the gods." Conversely, it is said that "Indra casts into the pit those who offer no sacrifice,"[4] and that "the wicked, who are false in thought and false in speech, are born for the deep abyss of hell."[5] In the following hymn

---

[1] Mandala i. Sukta 125, § 5.

[2] Wilson, "Rig-Veda," vol. i. p. 80, note *a*.

[3] *Ibid.* vol. ii. p. 42.

[4] Mandala i. Sukta 121, § 13.

[5] Wilson's "Rig-Veda," vol. iii. p. 129, compared with Max Müller ("Chips," vol. i. p. 47).

there is, at any rate, clear evidence that the early Vedic poets had aspirations after immortality:

"Where there is eternal light, in the world where the sun is placed,
In that immortal, imperishable world, place me, O Soma.

Where King Vaivaswata reigns, where the secret place of heaven is,
Where the mighty waters are, there make me immortal.

Where life is free, in the third heaven of heavens,
Where the worlds are radiant, there make me immortal.

Where wishes and desires are, where the place of the bright sun is,
Where there is freedom and delight, there make me immortal.

Where there is happiness and delight, where joy and pleasure reside,
Where the desires of our heart are attained, there make me immortal."[1]

As thus, occasionally, the deeper problems of human existence were approached, and, as it were, just touched by the Vedic bards, so there were times when some of the more thoughtful among them, not content with the simple and childish polytheism that had been the race's first instinct, attempted to penetrate further into the mystery of the Divine existence, to inquire into the relations that subsisted among the various gods generally worshipped, and even to search out the origin of all things. "Who has seen," says one,[2] "the primeval being at the time of his being born, when that which had no essence bore that which had an essence? Where was the

---

[1] The translation is Prof. Max Müller's ("Chips," vol. i. p. 46).

[2] Wilson's "Rig-Veda," vol. ii. pp. 127, 128. Compare Max Müller, "Lectures on the Science of Religion," p. 46.

life, the blood, the soul of the world?   Who sent to
ask this from the sage that knew it?   Immature in
understanding, undiscerning in mind," he goes on to
say, " I inquire after those things which are hidden
even from the gods.   .   .   .   Ignorant, I inquire
of the sages who know, who is the Only One who
upheld the spheres ere they were created?"   After a
multitude of speculations, he concludes—" They call
him Indra, Mitra, Varuna, Agni—then he is the
beautiful-winged heavenly Garutmat: that which is
one, the wise give it many names—they call it Agni,
Yama, Matarisvan."[1]   Another is still bolder, and
plunges headlong into the deepest vortex of meta-
physics.   The following is a metrical version of his
poem :[2]

> " A time there was, when nothing that now is
> Existed—no, nor that which now is not ;
> There was no sky, there was no firmament.
> What was it that then covered up and hid
> Existence?   In what refuge did it lie?
> Was water then the deep and vast abyss,
> The chaos in which all was swallowed up?
> There was no Death—and therefore nought immortal.
> There was no difference between night and day.
> The one alone breathed breathless by itself:
> Nor has aught else existed ever since.
> Darkness was spread around ; all things were veiled
> In thickest gloom, like ocean without light.
> The germ that in a husky shell lay hid,
> Burst into life by its own innate heat.

---

[1] Max Müller, " Chips from a German Workshop," vol. i. p. 29.
[2] I have followed as closely as possible the prose translation of
Max Müller, given with an intermixed comment in his " History
of Ancient Sanskrit Literature," pp. 559–563.

Then first came Love upon it, born of mind,
Which the wise men of old have called the bond
'Twixt uncreated and created things.
Came this bright ray from heaven, or from below?
Female and male appeared, and Nature wrought
Below, above wrought Will. Who truly knows,
Who has proclaimed it to us, whence this world
Came into being? The great gods themselves
Were later born. Who knows then whence it came?
The Overseer, that dwells in highest heaven,
He surely knows it, whether He Himself
Was, or was not, the maker of the whole,
Or shall we say, that even He knows not?"

This poem, and the other prayers above quoted, are sufficient to show that among the Vedic poets there were at any rate some who, by God's grace, had raised themselves above the murky atmosphere in which they were born, had "sought the Lord, and felt after Him,"[1] had struggled out of polytheism into a conscious monotheism, and, although they could not without revelation solve the problem of existence, had gone far to realise the maint points of true religion; the existence of one eternal and perfect Being, the dependence of man on Him, the necessity of men leading holy lives if they would please Him, and the need, which even the best man has, of His mercy and forgiveness.

[1] Acts xvii. 27.

CHAPTER V.

THE RELIGION OF THE PHŒNICIANS AND CAR-
THAGINIANS.

"Le dieu des Phéniciens, comme de tous les panthéismes asia-
tiques, etait a la fois un et plusieurs."—LENORMANT, *Manuel
d'Histoire Ancienne*, vol. iii. p. 127.

IN discussing the religion of the Phœnicians and
Carthaginians, we have to deal with a problem
far more difficult than any which has yet occupied
us. No "sacred book," like the Rig-Veda the
Zendavesta or the "Ritual of the Dead," here
spreads before us its stores of knowledge, requiring
little more than patient study to yield up to us the
secrets which it is the object of our inquiry to dis-
cover. No extensive range of sculptures or paint-
ings exhibits to our eyes, as in Assyria, Greece, and
Egypt, the outward aspect of the worship, the forms
of the gods, the modes of approaching them, the
general character of the ceremonial. Nor has even
any ancient author, excepting one, treated expressly
of the subject in question, or left us anything that
can be called in any sense an account of the religion.
It is true that we do possess, in the "Evangelical
Preparation" of Eusebius, a number of extracts

130

from a Greek writer of the first or second century after Christ bearing on the matter, and regarded by some moderns[1] as containing an authentic exposition of the Phœnician teaching on a number of points, which, if not exactly religion, are at any rate connected with religion. But the work of Philo Byblius, from which Eusebius quotes, is so wild, so confused, so unintelligible, that it is scarcely possible to gather from it, unless by a purely arbitrary method of interpretation,[2] any distinct views whatsoever. Moreover, the work is confined entirely to cosmogony and mythology, two subjects which are no doubt included in "religion," as that term was understood in the ancient world, but which lie so much upon its outskirts, and so little touch its inner heart, that even an accurate and consistent exposition would go a very short way towards acquainting us with the real character of a religious system of which we knew only these portions. Add to this, that it is very doubtful whether Philo of Byblus reported truly what he found in the Phœnician originals which he professed to translate, or did not rather import into them his own philosophical notions, and his own theories of the relation borne by the Phœnician theology to that of other countries.

If, upon these grounds, we regard the fragments of Philo Byblius as untrustworthy, and as only to

[1] Especially Baron Bunsen. (See "Egypt's Place in Universal History," vol. iii. pp. 162–287.)

[2] Bunsen assumes that Philo's work contains three cosmogonies, quite distinct, of which the second and third contradict the first.

be used with the utmost caution, we are reduced to draw our knowledge of the Phœnician and Carthaginian religion from scattered and incidental notices of various kinds—from the allusions made to the subject by the writers of portions of the Old Testament, from casual statements occurring in classical authors, from inscriptions, from the etymology of names, and from occasional representations accompanying inscriptions upon stones or coins. Such sources as these " require," as has been well said,[1] the greatest care before they can be properly sifted and successfully fitted together ;" and they constitute at best a scanty and unsatisfactory foundation for a portraiture which, to have any value, must be drawn with some sharpness and definiteness.

One of the most striking features of the Phœnician polytheism—especially striking when we compare it with the systems which lay geographically the nearest to it, those of Egypt and Assyria—is its comparative narrowness. If we make a collection of the divine names in use either in Phœnicia Proper or in the Phœnician colonies, we shall find that altogether they do not amount to twenty. Baal, Ashtoreth, Melkarth, Moloch, Adonis, Dagon, Eshmun, Hadad, El, Elinn, Baaltis, Onca, Shamas, Sadyk, the Kabiri, exhaust pretty nearly the list of the native deities ; and if we add to these the divinities adopted from foreign countries, Tanith, Hammon, (=Ammon), and Osir (—Osiris), we shall still find the number of distinct names not to exceed eighteen.

[1] Max Müller, "Science of Religion," pp. 117–118.

This is a small number compared even with the pantheon of Assyria ; compared with that of Egypt, it is very remarkably scanty.

It may be added that there are grounds for doubting whether even the eighteen names above given were regarded by the Phœnicians themselves as designating really so many deities. We shall find, as we proceed, reason to believe, or to suspect, that in more than one case it is the very same deity who is designated by two or more of the sacred names.

The general character of the names themselves is remarkable. A large proportion of them are honorific titles, only applicable to real persons, and indicative of the fact that from the first the Phœnician people, like most other Semitic races, distinctly apprehended the personality of the Supreme Being, and intended to worship, not nature, but God in nature, not planets, or elements, or storm, or cloud, or dawn, or lightning, but a being or beings above and beyond all these, presiding over them, perhaps, and working through them, but quite distinct from them, possessing a real personal character. El signified "the strong," or "the powerful," [1] and in the cognate Hebrew took the article, and became *ha-El*, "the Strong One," He who alone has true strength and power and who therefore alone deserves to be called "strong" or "mighty." Eliun is "the Exalted," "the Most High," and is so translated in our authorised version of Genesis (xiv. 18), where Melchizedek, King of Salem, the well-known type of our blessed Lord,[2] is

---

[1] Max Müller, "Science of Religion," p. 177.
[2] See Psa. cx. 4 Heb. vii. 1–24

said to have been "the priest of the *most High* God," which is in the original, "priest of El-Eliun." Again, Sadyk is "the Just," "the Righteous," and is identical with the *Zedek* occurring as the second element in Melchizedek, which St. Paul, in the Epistle to the Hebrews (vii. 2), translates by "King of righteousness." Baal is "Lord," or "Master," an equivalent of the Latin *dominus*, and hence a term which naturally requires another after it, since a lord must be lord of something. Hence in Phœnician inscriptions[1] we find *Baal-Tsur*, "Lord of Tyre," *Baal-Tsidon*, "Lord of Zidon," *Baal-Tars*, "Lord of Tarsus," and the like. Hence also we meet with such words[2] as *Baal-berith*, "Lord of treaties," *Baal-peor*, "Lord of Peor" (a mountain), *Baal-zebub*, "Lord of flies," and *Beel-samin*,[3] "Lord of Heaven." Adonis, or more properly Adoni, for the S is merely the Greek nominatival ending, has nearly the same meaning as Baal, being the Phœnician equivalent of the Hebrew *Adonai*, the word ordinarily rendered "Lord" in our version of the Old Testament. Adoni, however, takes no adjunct, since it is most properly translated "my lord," "lord of me,"[4] and thus contains in itself the object of the lordship. Moloch is *melek*, "king," the initial element in Melchizedek; and it is this same word which appears a second time, with an ad-

[1] Gesenius, "Scripturæ Linguæque Phœniciæ Monumenta," pp. 96, 277, etc.

[2] Num. xxv. 3, 5; Judg. viii. 33; ix. 4; 2 Kings i. 3, 6.

[3] Philo Byblius in the "Fragmenta Historicorum Græcorum," vol. iii. p. 565.

[4] Gesenius. p. 400.

junct, in Melkarth, which is a contraction of *melek-kereth*, or rather *melek-qereth*,[1] which means "king of the city." Baaltis, or Baalti, is the feminine form of Baal, with the suffix found also in Adoni, and has the meaning of "my lady." The Greeks expressed the word most commonly by Beltis, but occasionally by Belthes,[2] and, through a confusion of the kindred labials *m* and *b*, by Mylitta.[3] The Kabiri are "the Great Ones," from *kabbir*, "great," which makes *kabbirim* in the plural.

It may be suspected, though it cannot be proved, that these various names, excepting the last, were originaily mere epithets of the One Eternal and Divine Being who was felt to rule the world, and that, whatever may have been the case elsewhere, the Phœnicians at any rate began with the monotheistic idea, whether that idea originated in the recesses of their own hearts or was impressed upon them from without by revelation. If El, Eliun, Sadyk, Baal, Adoni, Moloch, Melkarth, were all one, may not the same have been true of Dagon, Hadad, Eshmun, Shamas, etc.? nay, may not even the foreign gods, Hammon and Osir, have been understood to be simply additional epithets of the Most High, expressive of his attributes of inscrutability and omniscience?

A primary objection may seem to lie against this view in the fact that the Phœnicians recognised not only gods, but goddesses, the name Ashtoreth [4] belonging

---

[1] Gesenius p. 96. [2] Hesych. ad voc. βήλθης. [3] Herod. i. 131, 199.

[4] Baal and Ashtoreth appear first *distinctly* as Phœnician gods in 1 Kings xi. 5; but we may suspect that they bear the same

to the religion from the very earliest time to which we can trace it back, and Baaltis being placed by the side of Baal, apparently as a distinct and separate personage. But it has been argued that "the original conception of female deities differs among Semitic and Aryan nations," and that the feminine forms among the Semites "were at first intended only to express the energy or the collective powers of the deity, not a separate being, least of all a wife."[1] And this view is confirmed by passages in ancient inscriptions which seem to identify Phœnician gods and goddesses, as one in the inscription of Mesa, which speaks of Chemosh-Ashtar as a single deity, another in an inscription from Carthage in which Tanith is called Pen-Baal, or "the face of Baal,"[2] and a third, on the tomb of Eshmunazar, King of Sidon, where Ashtoreth herself is termed *Shem-Baal*, "the name of Baal."[3] If Ashtoreth and Tanith were merely aspects of Baal, if the Phœnician Supreme God was "androgynous,"[4] the fact that the religious system of the people admitted goddesses as well as gods, will not militate against its original monotheism.

A more vital objection may be taken from the two names, Eshmun and Kabiri. The Kabiri were the

character where they are mentioned in Judges ii. 13; x. 6. They appear as Syrian gods in the hieroglyphical inscriptions as early as Rameses II. (about B. C. 1350).

[1] Max Müller, "Science of Religion," p. 183.
[2] De Vogue, in the "Journal Asiatique" for 1867, p. 138.
[3] Max Müller, "Science of Religion," p. 184.
[4] "Speaker's Commentary," vol. i. p. 732.

sons of Sadyk; they were seven in number;[1] they were actual deities, the special gods of sailors; images of them adorned the prows of vessels. And Eshmun, the name of their brother, is a word signifying "eight," or the "eighth." It seems clear from this that the Phœnicians ultimately recognised at least eight gods; and if so, we must pronounce them polytheists.

At any rate, whether or no they were polytheists from the first, it cannot be doubted that they became such. When the Carthaginian introduced by Plautus into his "Pœnulus" commences his speech[2] with the words "Yth alonim v'alonuth sicarthi," which Plautus rightly renders by "Deos deasque veneror," or, "I worship the gods and goddesses," he expresses a genuine Phœnician sentiment. Baal and Ashtoreth, if originally one, were soon divided, were represented under different forms, and were worshipped separately. El, Eliun, Sadyk, Adonis, Melkarth, drifted off from their original moorings, and became distinct and separate gods, sometimes with a local character.[3] Dagon, Eshmun, Shamas, had perhaps been distinct from their first introduction, as had been the Kabiri, and perhaps some others. Thus a small pantheon was formed, amounting, even including the Kabiri, to no more than about fifteen or twenty divinities.

---

[1] "Philo Byblius," c. 5, § 8; Damascius ap. Phot. "Bibliothec." p. 573.

[2] Plaut. "Pœnul." Act v. § 1.

[3] Moloch became the special god of the Ammonites; Hadad, of the Syrians.

At the head of all clearly stood Baal and Ashtoreth, the great male and the great female principles. Baal, "the Lord" *par excellence*, was perhaps sometimes and in some places taken to be the
sun;[1] but this was certainly not the predominant
idea of any period; and it may be questioned whether
in the original seats of the nation it was ever entertained until after the Roman conquest. As Bel in
Babylonia was completely distinct from Shamas,[2] so
was Baal in Phœnicia.[3] The Greeks rendered Bel
and Baal, not by Apollo, but by Zeus;[4] and their
rendering was approved by Philo Byblius,[5] who, if
a Greek by extraction, was well-versed in Phœnician
lore, and a native of Byblus, a Phœnician town.
Baal seems really to have been the Supreme God.
His chief titles were *Baal-shamayin*, "the Lord of
heaven," *Baal-berith*, "the Lord of treaties," corresponding to the Grecian "Zeus Orkios," and *Bel-
ithan*,[6] "the aged Lord," with which we may compare the Biblical phrase, "the Ancient of days."[7]
He was also known in Numidia as "the eternal
king."[8] Baal was the god to whom we may almost
say that *most* Phœnicians were consecrated soon after
their birth, the names given to them being in almost

---

[1] See Gesenius, "Scrip. Phœnic. Mon.," pl. 21.

[2] See above, p. 52–57.

[3] The separate worship of Shamas, or the Sun, appears in 2
Kings xxiii. 5, and in Gesenius, p. 119.

[4] Herod. i. 181; Diod. Sic. ii. 9.

[5] Philo. Bybl , c. iv. § 14.

[6] Damasc. ap. Phot. "Bibliothec." cod. ccxlii. p. 559.

[7] Dan. vii. 9, 13.   [8] Gesenius, pp. 197, 202, 205.

a majority of cases compounded with Baal or Bal.[1] Dedicatory inscriptions are in general addressed to him, either singly,[2] or in conjunction with a goddess, who is most usually Tanith.[3]   Not unfrequently he is addressed as Baal-Ham-mon, or Baal in the charac-ter of the Egyptian god Ammon,[4] with whom he is thus identified, not unna-turally, since Ammon too was recognised as the Su-preme God, and addressed as Zeus or Jupiter.[5]

ASTARTE.

Ashtoreth, or Astarte, is a word whereof no satis-factory account has as yet been given.   It seems to have no Semitic deriva-tion, and may perhaps have been adopted by the Sem-ites from an earlier Hamitic population.   Originally a mere name for the energy or activity of God, Ashtoreth came to be regarded by the Phœnicians as a real female personage, a supreme goddess, on a par with Baal,[6] though scarcely

[1] Eth-baal (1 Kings xvi. 31), Merbal (Herod. vii. 98), Hannibal, Hasdrubal, Adherbal, Maharbal, are well-known instances.

[2] Gesenius, "Script. Phœn. Mon.," Nos. 3, 4, 49, 51, etc.

[3] *Ibid.* Nos. 46, 47, 48, and 50.

[4] *Ibid.* p. 172.

[5] Herod. ii. 42; Diod. Sic. i. 13; Plut. "De Isid. et Osir," s. 9.

[6] See the inscription in Gesenius' collection, numbered 81 (pl.

worshipped so generally. In the native mythology
she was the daughter of Uranos (heaven), and the
wife of El, or Saturn.[1] The especial place of her
worship in Phœnicia was Sidon.[2] In one of her aspects she represented the moon, and bore the head
of a heifer with horns curving in a crescent form,[3]
whence she seems to have been sometimes called
Ashtoreth Karnaim,[4] or, "Astarte of the two horns."
But, more commonly, she was a nature goddess,
" the great mother," the representation of the female
principle in nature, and hence presiding over the
sexual relation, and connected more or less with love
and with voluptuousness. The Greeks regarded
their Aphrodite, and the Romans their Venus, as
her equivalent. One of her titles was " Queen of
Heaven;" and under this title she was often worshipped by the Israelites.[5]

Melkarth has been regarded by some writers as
"only another form of Baal."[6] But he seems to
have as good a claim to a distinct personality as any
Phœnician deity after Ashtoreth and Baal. The
Greeks and Romans, who make Baal equivalent to
their Zeus or Jupiter, always identify Melkarth with
Hercules;[7] and in a bilingual inscription,[8] set up by

47), where Baal and Ashtoreth are joined together. Compare
Judg. ii. 13; x. 6.

[1] Philo Bybl. c. iv. § 12.

[2] See 1 Kings xi. 5, 33, and compare the inscription of Eshmunazar.

[3] Philo Byblius, c. v. § 1.   [4] Gen. xiv. 5.

[5] Jer. vii. 18; xliv. 25.   [6] Kenrick, "Phœnicia," p. 322.

[7] Herod. ii. 44; Philo Bybl. c. iv. § 19, etc.

[8] This inscription is given by Gesenius (pl. 6).

two natives of Tyre, this identification is endorsed and accepted. When Melkarth is qualified as *baal-Tsur,* " baal of Tyre," it is not meant that he was the Tyrian form of the god Baal, but that he was the special tutelary " lord" of the great Phœnician city. The word Melkarth, as already explained, means " king of the city," and the city intended was originally Tyre, though Melkarth would seem to have been in course of time regarded as a god of cities generally; and thus he was worshipped at Carthage, at Heraclea in Sicily, at Amathus in Cyprus, at Gades in Spain, and elsewhere.[1] In Numidia[2] he had the title of "great lord;" but otherwise there is little in the Phœnician monuments to define his attributes or fix his character. We must suppose that the Greeks traced in them certain resemblances to their own conception of Hercules; but it may be doubtful whither the resemblances were not rather fanciful than real.

That Dagon was a Phœnician god appears from many passages in the fragments of Philo Byblius,[3] though the Israelites would seem to have regarded him as a special Philistine deity.[4] There are indications,[5] however, of his worship having been spread

[1] See the inscriptions in Gesenius (pls. 14, 16, 17): and the coins of Heraclea (pl. 38), of Gades (pl. 40), and of Sextus (*ibid.*) in the same. On Amathus, see Hesychius and voc. **Malicha.**

[2] Gesenius, pl. 27, No. 65.

[3] Especially c. iv. §§ 2, 6, 15.

[4] Judg. xvi. 23; 1 Sam. v. 2–5; 1 Chron. x. 10.

[5] Berosus speaks of an early Babylonian god as bearing the name of O-dacon, which is, perhaps, Dagon with a prefix

widely through Western Asia in very early times; and its primitive source is scarcely within the range of conjecture. According to the general idea, the Phœnician Dagon was a Fish-god,[1] having the form described by Berosus, and represented so often in the Assyrian sculptures—"a form resembling that of a fish, but with a human head growing below the fish's, and with human feet growing alongside of the fish's tail and coming out from it."[2] Fish are common emblems upon the Phœnician coins;[3] and the word Dagon is possibly derived from *dag*, "a fish," so that the temptation to identify the deity with the striking form revealed to us by the Ninevite sculptures is no doubt considerable. It ought, however, to be borne in mind that there is nothing in the Scriptural description of the Philistine Dagon to suggest the idea that the image which fell on its face before the ark of the covenant had in any respect the form of a fish.[4] Nor do the Assyrian monuments connect the name of

Dagon is an element in the name of a primitive Chaldæan monarch, which is read as Ismi-Dagon. Asshur-izir-pal couples Dagon with Anu in his inscriptions, and represents himself as equally the votary of both. Da-gan is also found in the Assyrian remains as an epithet of Belus. (See the Author's "Ancient Monarchies," vol. i. p. 614; 2nd edition.).

[1] See Kenrick, "Phœnicia," p. 323; Layard, "Nineveh and Babylon," p. 343; "Speaker's Commentary," vol. ii. p. 201, etc.

[2] Beros. Fr. i § 3.

[3] Gesenius, "Script. Phœn. Monumenta," pls. 40 and 41.

[4] There is nothing in the original corresponding to "the fishy part," which is given in the margin of the Authorised Version. The actual words are, "only Dagon was left to him." The meaning is obscure.

Dagon, which they certainly contain,[1] with the Fish-deity whose image they present. That deity is Nin or Ninus.[2] Altogether, therefore, it must be pronounced exceedingly doubtful whether the popular idea has any truth at all in it; or whether we ought not to revert to the view put forward by Philo,[3] that the Phœnician Dagon was a "corn-god," and presided over agriculture.

Adonis, or Tammuz, which was probably his true name,[4] was a god especially worshipped at Byblus. He seems to have represented nature in its alternate decline and revival, whence the myth spoke of his death and restoration to life; the river of Byblus was regarded as annually reddened with his blood; and once a year, at the time of the summer solstice, the women of Phœnicia and Syria generally " wept for Tammuz."[5] Extravagant sorrow was followed after an interval by wild rejoicings in honour of his restoration to life; and the excitement attendant on these alternations of joy and woe led on by almost necessary consequence, with a people of such a temperament as the Syrians, to unbridled licence and excess. The rites of Aphaca, where Adonis had

---

[1] Sir H. Rawlinson in the Author's " Herodotus," vol. i. p. 614; 3rd edition,

[2] *Ibid.* p. 642.

[3] Philo Bybl. c. iv. § 2:—Δάγων, ὅ ἐστι Σίτων. Compare § 13, where Dagon is said to have discovered corn and invented the plough, whence he was regarded by the Greeks as equivalent to their Zeus Arotrios.

[4] Gesenius, " Script. Phœn. Mon." p. 400.

[5] Ezek. viii. 14.

his chief temple, were openly immoral, and when they were finally put down, exhibited every species of abomination characteristic of the worst forms of heathenism.[1]

El, whom Philo Byblius identifies with Kronos,[2] or Saturn, is a shadowy god compared with those hitherto described. In the mythology he was the child of heaven and earth, the brother of Dagon, and the father of a son whom he sacrificed.[3] His actual worship by the Phœnicians is not very well attested, but may be regarded as indicated by such names as Hanni-el, Kadml (=Kadmi-el), Enyl (=Eni-el) and the like.[4] He is said to have been identified with the planet Saturn by the Phœnicians;[5] and this may be true of the later form of the religion, though El originally can scarcely have been anything but a name of the Supreme God. It corresponded beyond a doubt to Il, in the system of the Babylonians, who was the head of the pantheon,[6] and the special god of Babel, or Babylon, which is expressed by *Bab-il,* "the gate of Il," in the inscriptions.[7]

[1] Euseb. "Vit. Constantin. Magn." iii. 55. Compare Kenrick, "Phœnicia," vol. i. p. 311.

[2] Philo Bybl. c. iv. § 2:— Ἤλον τον καὶ Κρονον. Compare § 10 and § 21.

[3] Philo Bybl. c. vi. § 3.

[4] Hanni-el-occurs in a Phœnician inscription (Gesen. p. 133). Cadmil is given as one of the Kabiri by the Scholiast on Apollonius Rhodius (i. 917). Enyl is mentioned as a king of Byblus by Arrian ("Exp. Alex." ii. 20).

[5] Philo Bybl. l. s. c.

[6] See above, p. 47.

[7] Sir H. Rawlinson in the Author's Herodotus," vol. i. p. 613.

That Shamas, or Shemesh, "the sun," was worshipped separately from Baal has been already mentioned. In Assyria and Babylonia he was one of the foremost deities;[1] and his cult among the Phœnicians is witnessed by such a name as Abed-Shemesh, which is found in two of the native inscriptions.[2]

Abed-Shemesh means "servant of Shemesh," as Obadiah means "servant of Jehovah," and Abdallah "servant of Allah"; and is an unmistakable evidence of the worship of Shemesh by the people who employed it as the parallel names are of the worship, respectively, of Jehovah and Allah,

THE SUN.

by Jews and Mohammedans. The sun-worship of the Phœnicians seems to have been accompanied by a use of " sun-images,"[3] of which we have perhaps a specimen in the accompanying figure, which occurs on a votive tablet found in Numidia,[4] although the tablet itself is dedicated to Baal. There was also connected with it a dedication to the sun-god of chariots and horses, to which a quasi-divine charac-

---

[1] The Author's "Herodotus," vol. i. pp. 631–634.

[2] Gesenius, Script. Phœn. Mon." pl. 9.

[3] This is given in the margin of 2 Chron. xiv. 5 and xxxiv. 4, as the proper translation of *khammanim*, which seem certainly to have been images of some kind or other.

[4] Gesenius, "Script. Phœn. Mon." pl. 21.

ter attached,[1] so that certain persons were from their
birth consecrated to the sacred horses, and given by
their parents the name of Abed-Susim, "servant of
the horses," as we find by an inscription from Cyprus.[2] It may be suspected that the Hadad or Hadar
of the Syrians[3] was a variant name of Shamas, perhaps connected with *adir*, "glorious," and if so, with
the Sepharvite god, Adrammelech.[4] Adodus, according to Philo Byblius, was in a certain sense
"king (*melek*) of the gods."

These latter considerations make it doubtful
whether the Moloch or Molech, who was the chief
divinity of the Ammonites,[5] and of whose worship
by the Phœnicians there are certain indications,[6] is
to be viewed as a separate and substantive god, or as
a form of some other, as of Shamas, or of Baal, or of
Melkarth, or even of El. Molech meaning simply
"king" is a term that can naturally be applied to
any "great god," and which may equally well designate each of the four deities just mentioned. Rites
like those of Molech belonged certainly to El and to
Baal;[7] and the name may be an abbreviation of

[1] See 2 Kings xxiii. 11.
[2] Gesenius, p. 130, and pl. 11, No. 9.
[3] Found under the form of Adodus in Philo Byblius (c. v. § 1).
[4] 2 Kings xvii. 31.
[5] See 1 Kings xi. 7.
[6] The names Bar-melek, Abed-melek, and Melek-itten, which
occur in Phœnician inscriptions (Gesenius, pp. 105, 130, 135),
imply a god who has either the proper name of Moloch, or is
worshipped as "the king."
[7] Diod. Sic. xx. 14; Porphyr. "De Abstinentia," ii. 56; Gesen.
"Script. Phœn. Mon." p. 153.

Melkarth,[1] or a title—the proper title—of Shamas. The fact that Philo has a Melich, whom he makes a distinct deity,[2] is of no great importance, since it is clear that he multiplies the Phœnician gods unnecessarily; and moreover, by explaining Melich as equivalent to Zeus Meilichios, he tends to identify him with Baal.[3] Upon the whole, Moloch seems scarcely entitled to be viewed as a distinct Phœnician deity. The word was perhaps not a proper name *in Phœnicia*, but retained its appellative force, and may have applied to more than one deity.

A similarly indefinite character attaches to the Phœnician Baaltis. Beltis was in Babylonian mythology a real substantive goddess, quite distinct and separate from Ishtar, Gula, and Zirbanit;[4] but Baaltis in Phœnicia had no such marked character. We hear of no temples of Baaltis; of no city where she was specially worshipped.[5] The word does not even occur as an element in Phœnician proper names, and if in use at all as a sacred name among the Phœnicians, must almost certainly have been a mere epithet of Ashtoreth,[6] who was in reality the *sole* native goddess. Lydus expressly states[7] that Blatta,

---

[1] Melkarth is frequently abbreviated in the Phœnician inscriptions, and becomes Melkar, Mokarth, and even Mokar. Hesychius says that at Amathus Hercules was called Malika.

[2] Philo Bybl. c. iii. § 9.

[3] Since he calls Baal Zeus Belus (c. iv. § 17).

[4] See above, p. 61.

[5] Philo makes her a "queen of Byblus" (c. v. § 5), but says nothing of her worship there.

[6] See Kenrick's "Phœnicia," p. 301.

[7] "De Mensibus," i. 19.

which is (like Mylitta) a corruption of Baalti, was
"a name given to Venus by the Phœnicians."

Sadyk again, whom we have mentioned as a distinct deity on the strength of statements in Philo
Byblius and Damascius,[1] scarcely appears as a separate object of worship, either in Phœnicia or elsewhere. The nearest approach to such an appearance
is furnished by the names Melchi-zedek, and Adoni-
zedek,[2] which may admit of the renderings, "Sadyk
is my king," "Sadyk is my lord." Sadyk has not
been found as an element in any purely Phœnician
name; much less is there any distinct recognition of
him as a god upon any Phœnician monument. We
are told that he was the father of Eshmun and the
Kabiri;[3] and as they were certainly Phœnician gods
we must perhaps accept Sadyk as also included
among their deities. From his name we may conclude
that he was a personification of the Divine Justice.

Eshmun is, next to Baal, Ashtoreth, and Melkarth, the most clearly marked and distinct presentation of a separate deity that the Phœnician remains
set before us. He was the especial god of Berytus
(*Beirut*),[4] and had characteristics which attached to
no other deity. Why the Greeks should have identified him with their Asclepias or Æsculapius,[5] is

1 Philo Byblius, c. iii. § 13; c. iv. § 16; etc. Damasc. ap.
Phot. "Bibliothec" p. 573.

2 See Gen. xiv. 18, and Josh. x. 1.

3 Philo Byblius, c. iii. § 14; c. iv. § 16.

4 See Damascius ap. Phot. "Bibliothec." p. 573.

5 This is done by Philo of Byblus (c. v. § 8), by Damascius
(l. s. c.), by Strabo (xvii. 14), and others.

not clear. He was the youngest son of Sadyk, and was a youth of great beauty, with whom Ashtoreth fell in love, as she hunted in the Phœnician forests. The fable relates how, being frustrated in her designs, she afterwards changed him into a god, and transported him from earth to heaven.[1] Thenceforth he was worshipped by the Phœnicians almost as much as Baal and Ashtoreth themselves. His name became a frequent element in the Phœnician proper names;[2] and his cult was taken to Cyprus, to Carthage, and to other distant colonies.

With Eshmun must be placed the Kabiri, who in the mythology were his brothers,[3] though not born of the same mother.[4] It is doubtful whether the Kabiri are to be regarded as originally Phœnician, or as adopted into the religion of the nation from without. The *word* appears to be Semitic;[5] but the ideas which attach to it seem to belong to a widespread superstition,[6] whereby the discovery of fire and the original working in metals were ascribed to

[1] Damascius, l. s. c.

[2] Eshmun-azar, whose tomb has been found at Sidon, is the best known instance; but the Phœnician inscriptions give also Bar-Eshmun, Han-Eshmun, Netsib-Eshmun, Abed-Eshmun, Eshmun-itten, and others. (See Gesenius, "Script. Phœn. Mon." p. 136.)

[3] Damascius, l. s. c. ; Philo Byblius, c. v. § 8.

[4] Philo Bybl. c. iv. § 16.

[5] See above, p. 150. Mr. Kenrick questions the derivation from *kabbir* ("Egypt of Herodotus," p. 287); but almost all other writers allow it.

[6] See Mr. Kenrick's "Notes on the Cabiri," in the work above mentioned, pp. 264–287.

strong, misshapen, and generally dwarfish deities, like Phthah in Egypt, Hephaistos and the Cyclopes in Greece, "Gav the blacksmith" in Persia, and the gnomes in the Scandinavian and Teutonic mythologies. According to Philo Byblius[1] and Damascius,[2] the Phœnician Kabiri were seven in number, and according to the Scholiast on Apollonius Rho-

COIN OF COSSURA.

dius,[3] the names of four of them were Axierus, Axiokersus, Axiokersa, and Cadmilus or Casmilus. Figures supposed to represent them, or some of them, are found upon Phœnician coins, as especially on those of Cossura,[4] which are exceedingly curious. The Kabiri were said to have invented ships;[5] and it is reasonable to regard them as represented by the Patæci of Herodotus,[6] which were pigmy figures placed by the Phœnicians on the prows of their war-galleys, no doubt as tutelary divinities. The Greeks compared the Kabiri with their own Castor and Pollux, who like them presided over navigation.[7]

Besides their original and native deities, the

[1] Philo Byblius, c. v. § 8.
[2] Damascius, l. s. c.
[3] Schol. ad Apoll. Rhod. "Argonautica," i. 915.
[4] See Gesenius, "Script. Phœn. Mon." pl. 39.
[5] Philo Byblius, c. iii. § 14.
[6] Herod. iii. 37.
[7] Horat. "Od." i. 3, 2 ; iii. 29, 64.

Phœnicians acknowledged some whom they had certainly introduced into their system from an external source, as Osiris, Ammon, and Tanith. The worship of Osiris is represented on the coins of Gaulos,[1] which was an early Phœnician settlement; and "Osir" (= Osiris) occurs not unfrequently as an element in Phœnician names,[2] where it occupies the exact place elsewhere assigned to Baal, Melkarth, and Ashtoreth. Ammon is found under the form Hammon in votive tab-

COIN OF GAULOS.

lets, but does not occur independently; it is always attached as an epithet to Baal.[3] Whether it determines the aspect of Baal to that of a "sun-god" may be questioned,[4] since the original idea of Ammon was as far as possible remote from that of a solar deity.[5] But, at any rate, the constant connection shows that the two gods were not really viewed as distinct, but that in the opinion of the Phœnicians their own Baal corresponded to the Ammon of the Egyptians, both alike representing the Supreme Being. Tanith has an important place in a number of the inscriptions, being given precedence over Baal

[1] Gesenius, pl. 40, A.

[2] *Ibid.* pp. 96, 110, 130, etc.

[3] *Ibid.* pp. 108, 168, 174, 175, 177, and Davis, "Carthage and her Remains," pl. opp. p. 256.

[4] This was the opinion of Gesenius ("Script. Phœn. Mon." p. 170); but his arguments upon the point are not convincing.

[5] See above, p. 19.

himself.[1] She was worshipped at Carthage, in Cyprus,[2] by the Phœnician settlers at Athens[3] and elsewhere; but we have no proof of her being acknowledged in Phœnicia itself. The name is connected by Gesenius with that of the Egyptian goddess Neith,[4] or Net; but it seems rather to represent the Persian Tanata, who was known as Tanaitis or Tanaïs, and also as Anaitis or Aneitis to the Greeks. Whether there was, or was not, a remote and original connection between the goddesses Neith and Tanata is perhaps open to question; but the form of the name Tanith, or Tanath,[5] shows that the Phœnicians adopted their goddess, not from Egypt, but from Persia. With regard to the character and attributes of Tanath, it can only be said that, while in most respects she corresponded closely with Ashtoreth, whom she seems to have replaced at Carthage, she had to a certain extent a more elevated and a severer aspect. The Greeks compared her not only to their Aphrodite, but also to their Artemis,[6] the huntress-

[1] See Gesenius, pp. 168, 174, 175, 177; Davis, "Carthage and her Remains," l. s. c.

[2] Gesenius, p. 151. Compare p. 146, where the true reading is possibly Abed-Tanith.

[3] *Ibid.* p. 113.   [4] *Ibid.* pp. 117, 118.

[5] "Tanath" is the natural rendering of the Phœnician word, rather than "Tanith," and is preferred by some writers. (See Davis, "Carthage and her Remains," pp. 274–276.)

[6] In a bilingual inscription given by Gesenius, the Phœnician Abed-Tanath becomes in the Greek "Artemidorous." Anaitis or Tanata is often called "the Persian Artemis." (See Plutarch, "Vit. Lucull." p. 24; Bochart, "Geographia Sacra," iv. 19; Pausan. iii. 16, § 6, etc)

deity whose noble form is known to us from many pure and exquisite statues. It may be suspected that the Carthaginians, dwelling in the rough and warlike Africa, revolted against the softness and effeminacy of the old Phœnician cult, and substituted Tanath for Ashtoreth, to accentuate their protest against religious sensualism.[1]

It seems to be certain that in Phœnicia itself, and in the adjacent parts of Syria, the worship of Ashtoreth was from the first accompanied with licentious rites. As at Babylon,[2] so in Phœnicia and Syria— at Byblus, at Ascalon, at Aphaca, at Hierapolis[3]— the cult of the great Nature-goddess "tended to encourage dissoluteness in the relations between the sexes, and even to sanctify impurities of the most abominable description."[4] Even in Africa, where an original severity of morals had prevailed, and Tanith had been worshipped "as a virgin with martial attributes," and with "severe, not licentious, rites,"[5] corruption gradually crept in; and by the time of Augustine[6] the Carthaginian worship of the "celestial goddess" was characterised by the same impurity as that of Ashtoreth in Phœnicia and Syria.

[1] See Davis's "Carthage," p. 264; Munter, "Religion des Karthager," c. 6.

[2] Herod. i. 199.

[3] Herod. i. 105; Lucian, "De Dea Syra," c. ix; Euseb. "Vit. Constantin. Magni," iii. 55.

[4] Twistleton, in Smith's "Dictionary of the Bible," vol. ii. p. 866.

[5] Kenrick, "Phœnicia," p. 305.

[6] Augustine, "De Civitate Dei," ii. 4.

Another fearful blot on the religion of the Phœnicians, and one which belongs to Carthage quite as much as to the mother-country,[1] is the systematic offering of human victims, as expiatory sacrifices, to El and other gods. The ground of this horrible superstition is to be found in the words addressed by Balak to Balaam[2]—" Wherewith shall I come before the Lord, and bow myself before the high God? Shall I come before Him with burnt offerings, with calves of a year old? Will the Lord be pleased with thousands of rams, or with ten thousands of rivers of oil? *Shall I give my firstborn for my transgression, the fruit of my body for the sin of my soul?*" As Philo Byblius expresses it,[3] " It was customary among the ancients, in times of great calamity and danger, that the rulers of the city or nation should offer up the best beloved of their children, as an expiatory sacrifice to the avenging deities: and these victims were slaughtered mystically." The Phœnicians were taught that, once upon a time, the god El himself, under the pressure of extraordinary peril, had taken his only son, adorned him with royal attire, placed him as a victim upon an altar, and slain him with his own hand. Thenceforth, it could not but be the duty of rulers to follow the divine example set them; and even private indi-

---

[1] See Diod. Sic. xx. 14, 65; Justin, xviii. 6; Sil. Ital. iv. 765-768; Dionys. Hal. i. 38; etc. Compare Gesenius, "Script. Phœn. Mon." pp. 448, 449, 453; and Davis, "Carthage," pp. 296, 267.

[2] Micah vi. 6, 7.

[3] Philo Bybl., c. vi. § 3.

viduals, when beset by difficulties, might naturally apply the lesson to themselves, and offer up their children to appease the divine anger. We have only too copious evidence that both procedures were in vogue among the Phœnicians. Porphyry declares[1] that "the Phœnician history was full of instances, in which that people, when suffering under great calamity from war, or pestilence, or drought, chose by public vote one of those most dear to them, and sacrificed him to Saturn." Two hundred noble youths were offered on a single occasion at Carthage, after the victory of Agathocles.[2] Hamilcar, it is possible, offered himself as a victim on the entire defeat of his army by Gelo.[3] When Tyre found itself unable to resist the assault of Alexander the Great, the proposition was made, but overruled, to sacrifice a boy to Saturn.[4] Every year, at Carthage, there was at least one occasion, on which human victims, chosen by lot, were publicly offered to expiate the sins of the nation.[5]

And private sacrifices of this sort went hand in hand with public ones. Diodorus tell us,[6] that in the temple of Saturn at Carthage, the brazen image of the god stood with outstretched hands to receive the bodies of children offered to it. Mothers brought their infants in their arms; and, as any manifestation

[1] "De Abstinentia," ii. 56.

[2] Lactant. "Inst." i. 21, quoting Pescennius Festus.

[3] See the story in Herodotus (vii. 167).

[4] Quint. Curt. "Vit. Alex. Magn." iv. 15.

[5] Silius Ital. iv. 765–768.

[6] Diod. Sic. xx. 14.

of reluctance would have made the sacrifice unacceptable to the god, stilled them by their caresses till the moment when they were handed over to the image, which was so contrived as to consign whatever it received to a glowing furnace underneath it. Inscriptions found at Carthage record the offering of such sacrifices.[1] They continued even after the Roman conquest; and at length the proconsul Tiberius, in order to put down the practice, hanged the priests of these bloody rites on the trees of their own sacred grove.[2] The public exhibitions of the sacrifice thenceforth ceased, but in secret they still continued down to the time of Tertullian.[3]

The Phœnicians were not idolaters, in the ordinary sense of the word; that is to say, they did not worship images of their deities. In the temple of Melkarth at Gades there was no material emblem of the god at all, with the exception of an ever-burning fire.[4] Elsewhere, conical stones, called *bætyli*, were dedicated to the various deities,[5] and received a certain qualified worship, being regarded as possessed

---

[1] Gesenius, "Script. Phœn. Mon.," pp. 448, 449. An inscription given by Dr. Davis ("Carthage and her Remains," pp. 296, 297) refers to the public annual sacrifice.

[2] Tertull. "Apologia," c. ix.

[3] *Ibid.*

[4] Silius Ital. ii. 45.

[5] Philo Bybl. c. iv. § 2; Damasc. ap. Phot. "Bibliothec." p. 1065; Hesych. ad voc. Βαίτυλος. It has been proposed to explain the word *bætulus* as equivalent to Beth-el, "House of God," and to regard the Phœnicians as believing that a deity dwelt in the stone. (Kenrick, "Phœnicia," p. 323, note 4.)

of a certain mystic virtue.[1] These stones seem occasionally to have been replaced by pillars, which were set up in front of the temples, and had sacrifices offered to them.[2] The pillars might be of metal, of stone, or of wood, but were most commonly of the last named material, and were called by the Jews *asherahs*, "uprights."[3] At festive seasons they seem to have been adorned with boughs of trees, flowers, and ribands, and to have formed the central object of a worship which was of a sensual and debasing character. An emblem common in the Assyrian sculptures is thought to give a good idea of the ordinary appearance on such occasions of these *asherahs*.

SACRED TREE—ASHERAH.

Worship was conducted publicly in the mode usual

[1] The original *bætuli* were perhaps aeroliths, which were regarded as divine, since they had fallen from the sky.

[2] Philo Byblius, c. iii. § 7. On the pillar-worship of the Phœnicians, see Bunsen, Egypt's Place in Univ. History," vol. iv. pp. 208–212.

[3] *Asherah* is commonly translated by "grove" in the Authorised Version; but its true character has been pointed out by many critics. (See "Speaker's Commentary," vol. i. pp. 416, 417; "Ancient Monarchies," vol. ii. p. 8; 2nd edition.)

in ancient times, and comprised praise, prayer and
sacrifice. The victims offered were ordinarily animals,[1]
though, as already shown, human sacrifices were not
infrequent. It was usual to consume the victims entirely upon the altars.[2] Libations of wine were copiously poured forth in honour of the chief deities,[3] and
incense was burnt in lavish profusion.[4] Occasionally
an attempt was made to influence the deity invoked by
loud and prolonged cries, and even by self-inflicted
wounds and mutilation.[5] Frequent festivals were held,
especially one at the vernal equinox, when sacrifices
were made on the largest scale, and a vast concourse
of persons was gathered together at the chief temples.[6]
Altogether the religion of the Phœnicians, while
possessing some redeeming points, as the absence of
images and deep sense of sin which led them to
sacrifice what was nearest and dearest to them to
appease the divine anger, must be regarded as one
of the lowest and most debasing of the forms of
belief and worship prevalent in the ancient world,
combining as it did impurity with cruelty, the sanction of licentiousness with the requirement of bloody
rites, revolting to the conscience, and destructive of
any right apprehension of the true idea of God.

[1] Lucian, "De Dea Syra," § 49.
[2] Gesenius, "Script. Phœn. Mon." pp. 446, 447; Movers, "Das
Opferwesen der Karthager," p. 71, etc.
[3] Philo Bybl. c. iv. § 1.
[4] Virg. "Æn." i. 415.
[5] 1 Kings xviii. 26, 28; Lucian, "De Dea Syra," § 50; Plutarch, "De Superstitione," p. 170, c.
[6] Lucian, "De Dea Syra," § 49.

CHAPTER VI.

THE RELIGION OF THE ETRUSCANS.

" Hetrusci, religione imbuti."—*Cic. De Div.* i. 42.

THE religion of the Etruscans, or Tuscans, like
that of the Phœnicians and Carthaginians, is
known to us chiefly from the notices of it which
have come down to us in the works of the classical
writers, Greek and Latin. It has, however, the
advantage of being illustrated more copiously than
the Phœnician by monuments and other works of art
found in the country, the productions of native
artists—works which in some respects give us a considerable insight into its inner character. On the
other hand, but little light is thrown upon it by the
Etruscan inscriptions, partly because these inscriptions are almost all of a single type, being short
legends upon tombs, partly from the fact that the
Etruscan language has defied all the efforts made to
interpret it, and still remains, for the most part, an
insoluble, or at any rate an unsolved, problem. We
are thus without any genuine Etruscan statements of
their own views upon religious subjects, and are
forced to rely mainly upon the reports of foreigners,
who looked upon the system only from without, and

159

are not likely to have fully understood it. It is a further disadvantage that our informants write at a time when the Etruscans had long ceased to be a nation, and when the people, having been subjected for centuries to foreign influences, had in all probability modified their religious views in many important points.

There seems to be no doubt that their religion, whatever it was, occupied a leading position in the thoughts and feelings of the Etruscan nation. "With Etruria," says a modern writer, "religion was an all-pervading principle—the very atmosphere of her existence—a leaven operating on the entire mass of society, a constant pressure ever felt in one form or other, a power admitting no rival, all-ruling, all-regulating, all-requiring.[1] Livy calls the Etruscans "a race which, inasmuch as it excelled in the art of religious observances, was more devoted to them than any other nation." [2] Arnobius says that Etruria was "the creator and parent of superstition." [3] The very name of the nation, Tusci, was derived by some from a root, *thucin*, "to sacrifice," or "make offerings to the gods" [4]—as if that were the chief occupation of the people. While famous among the nations of antiquity for their art, their commerce, and their warlike qualities, the Etruscans were

[1] Dennis, "Cities and Cemeteries of Etruria, vol. i. Introduction, p. xlix.

[2] "Gens ante omnes alias eo magis dedita religionibus, quod excelleret arte colendi eas," Liv. v. 1.

[3] Arnob. "Adv. Gentes," vii.

[4] Servius, "Comment. in Virg. Æn." x. 1. 257.

above all else celebrated for their devotion to their religion, and for "the zeal and scrupulous care with which they practised the various observances of its rites and ceremonies."[1]

The objects of worship were twofold, including (1) Deities proper, and (2) the Lares, or ancestral spirits of each family. The deities proper may be divided into three classes : first, those whose sphere was the heaven, or some portion of it ; secondly, those who belonged more properly to earth ; and thirdly, those of the infernal regions, or nether world, which held a prominent place in the system, and was almost as much in the thoughts of the people as their "Amenti" was in the thoughts of the Egyptians.[2]

The chief deities of the Heaven were the following five : Tina, or Tinia, Cupra, Menrva, Usil and Losna.

Tina, or Tinia, who was recognised as the chief god,[3] and whom the Greeks compared to their Zeus, and the Romans to their Jupiter, seems to have been originally the heaven itself, considered in its entirety, and thus corresponded both in name and nature to the Tien of the Chinese, with whom it may be suspected that the Etruscans had some ethnic affinity. Tina is said to have had a special temple dedicated to his honour in every Etruscan city, and in every

[1] Smith, "Dictionary of Greek and Roman Geography," vol. i p. 865.

[2] See above, p. 33.

[3] Dennis, "Cities and Cemeteries," vol. i. "Introduction," p. 1 ; Taylor, "Etruscan Researches," p. 132.

11

such city one of the gates bore his name.[1]   He appears to have been sometimes worshipped under the
appellation of Summanus, which perhaps meant " the
supreme god."[2]   We must not, however, take this
term as indicative of a latent monotheism, whereof
there is no trace in the Etruscan religion, but only
as a title of honour, or at most as a recognition of a
superiority in rank and dignity on the part of this
god, who was *primus inter pares,* the presiding spirit
in a conclave of equals.

Next to Tina came Cupra, a goddess, who appears
to have also borne the name of Thalna or Thana.[3]
The Greeks compared her to their Hera, and the
Romans to their Juno, or sometimes to their Diana,
who was originally the same deity.   Like Tina,
Cupra had a temple in every Etruscan city, and a
gate named after her.[4]   It is thought by some that
she was a personification of light, or day ;[5] but this
is uncertain.   Her name, Thana, looks like a mere
variant of Tina, and would seem to make her a mere
feminine form of the sky-god, his complement and
counterpart, standing to him as Amente to Ammon
in the Egyptian, or as Luna to Lunus in the Roman
mythology.   A similar relation is found to have sub-

---

[1] Servius, " Comment in Virg. Æn." i. 422.

[2] Max Müller, " Science of Religion," p. 376.

[3] The name Cupra is known to us only from Strabo ("Geo-
graph." v. p. 241).   Thalna is found on Etruscan monuments.

[4] Servius, l. s. c.

[5] Gerhard, " Gottheiten der Etrusker," p. 40 ; Taylor, " Etruscan Researches," p. 142.

sisted between the two chief deities of the Etruscan nether world.

The third among the celestial deities was Menrva, or Menrfa, out of whom the Romans made their Minerva. She enjoyed the same privileges in the Etruscan cities as Tina and Cupra, having her own temple and her own gate in each of them.[1] Mr. Isaac Taylor believes that originally she represented the half light of the morning and evening, and even ventures to suggest that her name signified "the red heaven," and referred to the flush of the sky at dawn and sunset.[2] A slight confirmation is afforded to this view by the fact that we sometimes find *two* Menrvas represented in a single Etruscan work of art.[3] But we scarcely possess sufficient materials for determining the real original character of this deity. It was probably foreign influence that brought her ultimately into that close resemblance which she bears to Minerva and Athênê on the mirrors and vases, where she is represented as armed and bearing the ægis.[4]

Usil and Losna, whom we have ventured to join with Tina, Cupra, and Menrva as celestial deities, appear to have been simply the Sun and the Moon, objects of worship to so many ancient nations. Usil was identified with the Greek Apollo (called Aplu by the Etruscans), and was represented as a youth with

[1] Servius, 1. s. c.
[2] " Etruscan Researches," p. 137.
[3] *Ibid.* p. 138.
[4] Dennis, " Cities and Cemeteries," vol. i. Introduction, p. li.

bow and arrows.[1] Losna had the crescent for her
emblem,[2] and was figured nearly as Diana by the
Romans.[3]

Next to Usil and Losna may be placed in a group
the three elemental gods, Sethlans, the god of fire,
identified by the Etruscans themselves with the
Greek Hephaistos and the Latin Vulcan; Nethuns,
the water-god, probably the same as Neptunus; and
Phuphlans, the god of earth and all earth's products,
who is well compared with Dionysus and Bacchus.[4]
Phuphlans was the special deity of Pupluna, or (as
the Romans called it) Populonia.[5] He seems to have
been called also Vortumnus or Volturnus;[6] and in
this aspect he had a female counterpart, Voltumna,
whose temple was the place of meeting where the
princes of Etruria discussed the affairs of the Con-
federation.[7]

Another group of three consists of Turan, Thesan,
and Turms, native Etruscan deities, as it would seem,
corresponding more or less closely to the Aphrodite,
Eos, and Hermes of the Greeks, and the Venus,
Aurora, and Mercurius of the Romans. Of these
Turan is the most frequently found, but chiefly in
subjects taken from the Greek mythology, while

1 Taylor, "Etruscan Researches." p. 143.
2 Lanzi, "Saggio della Lingua Etrusca," vol. ii. p. 76.
3 Dennis, "Cities and Cemeteries," vol. i. Introduction, p. liv.
4 Taylor, "Etruscan Researches," p. 141; Smith, "Dict. of
Greek and Rom. Antiquities," vol. i. p. 865.
5 Dennis, "Cities and Cemeteries," vol. ii. p. 242.
6 *Ibid.* vol. i. Introduction, p. liii.
7 Liv. iv. 23, 61; v. 17, etc.

Thesan occurs the least often. According to one view, the name Turms is the mere Etruscan mode of writing the Greek word Hermes,[1] the true native name having been Camillus or Kamil.[2] It does not appear that any of these three gods was much worshipped by the Etruscans. They figured in the mythology, but lay almost outside the religion.

The main character in which the gods of heaven and earth were recognised by the Etruscans was that of rulers, signifying, and sometimes executing, their will by means of thunder and lightning. Nine great gods, known as the Novensiles, were believed to have the power of hurling thunderbolts, and were therefore held in special honour.[3] Of these nine, Tinia, Cupra, Menrva, and Sethlans, were undoubtedly four. Summanus and Vejovis, who are sometimes spoken of as thundering gods,[4] seem to be mere names or aspects of Tinia. The Etruscans recognised twelve sorts of thunder-bolts, and ascribed, we are told, to Tinia three of them.[5]

But it was to the unseen world beneath the earth, the place to which men went after death, and where the souls of their ancestors resided, that the Etruscans devoted the chief portion of their religious thought; and with this were connected the bulk of their religious observances. Over the dark realms of the dead

[1] Taylor, "Etruscan Researches," p. 149.

[2] So Callimachus ap. Serv. in Virg. Æn. xi. 1. 543.

[3] Varro, "De Ling. Lat." v. 74; Plin. "H. N." ii. 53; Manilius ap. Arnob. "Adv. Gentes," iii. 38.

[4] Plin. l. s. c.; Amm. Marc. xvii. 10, § 2.

[5] Senec. "Nat. Quæst." ii. 41.

ruled Mantus and Mania, king and queen of Hades,
the former represented as an old man, wearing a
crown, and with wings on his shoulders, and bearing
in his hands sometimes a torch, sometimes two or
three large nails, which are thought to indicate "the
inevitable character of his decrees."[1]   Intimately connected with these deities, their prime minister and
most active agent, cruel, hideous, half human, half
animal, the chief figure in almost all the representations of the lower world, is the demon, Charun, in
name no doubt identical with the Stygian ferryman
of the Greeks, but in character so different that it has
even been maintained that there is no analogy between
them.[2]   Charun is "generally represented as a squalid
and hideous old man with flaming eyes and savage
aspect; but he has, moreover, the ears, and often the
tusks of a brute," with (sometimes) "negro features
and complexion, and frequently wings,"[3] so that he
"answers well, cloven feet excepted, to the modern
conception of the devil."   His brow is sometimes
bound round by snakes; at other times he has a snake
twisted round his arm; and he bears in his hands
almost universally a huge mallet or hammer, up-
raised, as if he were about to deal a death-stroke.
When death is being inflicted by man, he stands by,
"grinning with savage delight;"[4] when it comes

---

[1] Dennis, "Cities and Cemeteries," vol. i. Introduction, p. lvi.

[2] Ambrosch, "De Charonte Etrusco," quoted by Dennis, vol.
ii. p. 206.

[3] Dennis, "Cities and Cemeteries," vol. ii. p. 206.

[4] *Ibid.* p. 207.

naturally, he is almost as well pleased; he holds the horse on which the departed soul is to take its journey to the other world, bids the spirit mount, leads away the horse by the bridle or drives it before him, and thus conducts the deceased into the grim kingdom of the dead.[1] In that kingdom he is one of the tormentors of guilty souls, whom he strikes with his mallet, or with a sword, while they kneel before him and implore for mercy. Various attendant demons and furies, some male, some female, seem to act under his orders, and inflict such tortures as he is pleased to prescribe.

It must be supposed that the Etruscan conceived of a judgment after death, and of an apportionment of rewards and punishments according to desert.[2] But it is curious that the representations in the tombs give no clear evidence of any judicial process, containing nothing analogous to the Osirid trial, the weighing of the soul, the sentence, and the award accordingly, which are so conspicuous on the monuments of Egypt. Good and evil spirits seem to contend for the possession of souls in the nether world; furies pursue some, and threaten them or torment them; good genii protect others and save them from the dark demons, who would fain drag them to the place of punishment.[3] Souls are represented in a state which seems to be intended for one of ideal

---

[1] Dennis, "Cities and Cemeteries," pp. 193, 194.

[2] So Dennis and others; but there is a want of distinct evidence upon the point.

[3] Dennis, "Cities and Cemeteries," vol. ii. pp. 193-198.

happiness, banqueting, or hunting, or playing at games, and otherwise enjoying themselves;[1] but the grounds of the two different conditions in which the departed spirits exist are not clearly set forth, and it is analogy rather than strict evidence which leads us to the conclusion that desert is the ground on which the happiness and misery are distributed.

Besides Charun and his nameless attendant demons and furies, the Etruscan remains give evidence of a belief in a certain small number of genii, or spirits, having definite names, and a more or less distinct and peculiar character. One of the most clearly marked of these is Vanth, or Death, who appears in several of the sepulchral scenes, either standing by the door of an open tomb, or prompting the slaughter of a prisoner, or otherwise encouraging carnage and de-struction.[2] Another is Kulmu, "god of the tomb," who bears the fatal shears in one hand and a funeral torch in the other, and opens the door of the sepul-chre that it may receive into it a fresh inmate.[3] A third being of the same class is Nathuns, a sort of male fury, represented with tusk-like fangs and hair standing on end, while in either hand he grasps a serpent by the middle, which he shakes over avengers, in order to excite them to the highest pitch of frenzy.[4]

[1] Dennis, "Cities and Cemeteries," vol. i. pp. 444–446.

[2] Taylor, "Etruscan Researches," pp. 100–102. (For the scenes referred to, see Micali, "Monumenti Inediti," pl. lx.; and Des Vergers, "L'Etrurie et les Etrusques," pl. xxi.).

[3] *Ibid.* p. 94.

[4] Taylor, "Etruscan Researches," p. 112.

In their worship the Etruscans sought, first of all and especially, to know the will of the gods, which they believed to be signified to man in three principal ways. These were thunder and lightning, which they ascribed to the direct action of the heavenly powers; the flight of birds, which they supposed to be subject to divine guidance; and certain appearances in the entrails of victims offered in sacrifice, which they also regarded as supernaturally induced or influenced. To interpret these indications of the divine will, it was necessary to have a class of persons trained in the traditional knowledge of the signs in question, and skilled to give a right explanation of them to all inquirers. Hence the position of the priesthood in Etruria, which was "an all-dominant hierarchy, maintaining its sway by an arrogant exclusive claim to intimate acquaintance with the will of heaven, and the decrees of fate."[1] The Etruscan priests were not, like the Egyptian, the teachers of the people, the inculcators of a high morality, or the expounders of esoteric doctrines on the subjects of man's relation to God, his true aim in life, and his ultimate destiny; they were soothsayers,[2] who sought to expound the future, immediate or remote, to warn men against coming dangers, to suggest modes of averting the divine anger, and thus to save men from

[1] Dennis, "Cities and Cemeteries," vol. i. Introduction, p. xxxix.

[2] Cic. "De Divinatione," i. p. 41, 42; Senec. "Nat. Quæst." ii. 32; Diod. Sic. v. p. 316; Dionys. Hal. ix. p. 563; Aulus Gell. iv. 5; Lucan, "Phars." i. 1. 587. etc.

evils which would otherwise have come upon them unawares and ruined or, at any rate, greatly injured them. Men were taught to observe the signs in the sky, and the appearance and flight of birds, the sounds which they uttered, their position at the time, and various other particulars; they were bidden to note whatever came in their way that seemed to them unusual or abnormal, and to report all to the priests, who thereupon pronounced what the signs observed portended, and either announced an inevitable doom,[1] or prescribed a mode whereby the doom might be postponed or averted. Sometimes the signs reported were declared to affect merely individuals; but frequently the word went forth that danger was portended to the state; and then it was for the priesthood to determine at once the nature and extent of the danger, and also the measures to be adopted under the circumstances. Sacrifices on a vast scale or of an unusual character were commonly commanded in such cases, even human victims being occasionally offered to the infernal deities, Mantus and Mania,[2] whose wrath it was impossible to appease in any less fearful way. Certain books in the possession of the hierarchy, ascribed to a half divine,

[1] The Etruscans recognised a power of Fate, superior to the great gods themselves, Tinia and the others, residing in certain " Di Involuti," or " Di Superiores," who were the rulers of both gods and men (Senec. " Nat. Quæst." ii. 41).

[2] Especially to Mania (Macrob. "Saturnalia," i. 7). Human sacrifices are thought to be represented in the Etruscan remains (Dennis, "Cities and Cemeteries," vol. ii. pp. 190, 191).

half human personage, named Tages,[1] and handed
down from a remote antiquity, contained the system
of divination which the priests followed, and guided
them in their expositions and requirements.

Among sacrificial animals were included the bull,
the ass, and perhaps the wolf,[2] though this is disputed. The victim, brought by an individual citi-
zen, was always offered by a priest, and libations
usually accompanied the sacrifice. Unbloody offerings were also not unfrequently presented, and were
burnt upon the altar, like the victims.[3]

A general survey of the Etruscan remains has
convinced the most recent inquirers, that the public
worship of the gods in the temples, which were to be
found in all Etruscan cities, by sacrifice, libation, and
adoration, played but a very small part in the religious life of the nation. "The true temples of the
Etruscans," it has been observed, "were their
tombs."[4] Practically, the real objects of their worship were the Lares, or spirits of their ancestors.
Each house probably had its *lararium*,[5] where the
master of the household offered prayer and worship

[1] Lydus, "De Ostentis," § 27; Cic. "De Div." ii. 23; Ovid.
"Metamorph." xv. 553–559, etc.

[2] Dennis, "Cities and Cemeteries," vol. ii. pp. 189, 190.

[3] Dennis, "Cities and Cemeteries," vol. ii. p. 191.

[4] Taylor, "Etruscan Researches," p. 49.

[5] On the Roman *lararium*, which is believed to have been
adopted from the Etruscans, see an article in Dr. Smith's "Dictionary of Greek and Roman Antiquities," pp. 667, 668, 2nd
edition.

every morning, and sacrifice occasionally.[1] And each
family certainly had its family tomb, constructed on
the model of a house, in which the spirits of its
ancestors were regarded as residing. " The tombs
themselves," we are told, "are exact imitations of
the house. There is usually an outer vestibule,
apparently appropriated to the annual funeral feast:
from this a passage leads to a large central chamber,
which is lighted by windows cut through the rock.
The central hall is surrounded by smaller chambers,
in which the dead repose. On the roof we see carved
in stone the broad beam, or roof-tree, with rafters
imitated in relief on either side, and even imitations
of the tiles. These chambers contain the corpses,
and are furnished with all the implements, ornaments, and utensils used in life. The tombs are, in
fact, places for the dead to live in. The position and
surroundings of the deceased are made to approxi-
mate as closely as possible to the conditions of life.
The couches on which the corpses repose have a tri-
clinial arrangement, and are furnished with cushions
carved in stone; and imitations of easy-chairs and
footstools are carefully hewn out of the rock. Everything, in short, is arranged as if the dead were reclining at a banquet in their accustomed dwellings. On
the floor stand wine-jars; and the most precious
belongings of the deceased—arms, ornaments, and

[1] In the Theodosian Code it was provided that no one should
any longer worship his *lar* with fire ("nullus Larem igne vene-
retur"), or, in other words, continue to sacrifice to him. (See
Keightley's "Mythology," p. 470.)

mirrors—hang from the roof, or are suspended on the walls. The walls themselves are richly decorated, usually being painted with representations of festive scenes; we see figures in gaily-embroidered garments reclining on couches, while attendants replenish the goblets, or beat time to the music of the pipers. Nothing is omitted which can conduce to the amusement or comfort of the deceased. Their spirits were evidently believed to inhabit these house-tombs after death, just as in life they inhabited their houses." [1]

The tombs were not permanently closed. Once a year at least, perhaps oftener, it was customary for the surviving relatives to visit the resting-place of their departed dear ones, to carry them offerings as tokens of affectionate regard, and solicit their favour and protection. The presents brought included portrait-statues, cups, dishes, lamps, armour, vases, mirrors, gems, seals, and jewellery. [2] Inscriptions frequently accompanied the offerings; and these show that the gifts were made, not to the spirit of the tomb, or to the infernal gods, or to any other deities, but to the persons whose remains were deposited in the sepulchres. [3] Their spirits were no doubt regarded as conciliated by the presents; and, practically, it is probable that far more value was attached to the

[1] Taylor, " Etruscan Researches," pp. 46–48.

[2] *Ibid.* pp. 271, 306, etc.

[3] Without accepting all Mr. Taylor's renderings of the funereal inscriptions, I am of opinion that he has succeeded in establishing this point.

fostering care of these nearly allied protectors than to the favour of the awful gods of earth and heaven, who were distant beings, dimly apprehended, and chiefly known as wielders of thunderbolts.

As a whole, the Etruscan religion must be pronounced one of the least elevating of the forms of ancient belief. It presented the gods mainly under a severe and forbidding aspect, as beings to be dreaded and propitiated, rather than loved and worshipped. It encouraged a superstitious regard for omens and portents, which filled the mind with foolish alarms, and distracted men from the performance of the duties of every-day life. It fostered the pride and vanity of the priestly class by attributing to them superhuman wisdom, and something like infallibility, while it demoralised the people by forcing them to cringe before a selfish and arrogant hierarchy. If it diminished the natural tendency of men to overvalue the affairs of this transitory life, by placing prominently before them the certainty and importance of the life beyond the grave, yet its influence was debasing rather than elevating, from the coarseness of the representations which it gave alike of the happiness and misery of the future state. Where the idea entertained of the good man's final bliss makes it consist in feasting and carousing,[1] and the

[1] See Dennis, "Cities and Cemeteries," vol. i. p. 294: "They (the Etruscans) believed in the materiality of the soul; and their Elysium was but a glorification of the present state of existence; the same pursuits, amusements, and pleasures they had relished in this life they expected in the next, but divested of their sting, and enhanced by increased capacities of enjoyment. To cele-

suffering of the lost arises from the blows and wounds inflicted by demons, the doctrine of future rewards and punishments loses much of its natural force, and is more likely to vitiate than to improve the moral character. The accounts which we have of the morality of the Etruscans are far from favourable;[1] and it may be questioned whether the vices whereto they were prone did not receive a stimulus, rather than a check, from their religion.

brate the great event, to us so solemn (i. e., death), by feasting and joviality, was not with them unbecoming. They knew not how to conceive or represent a glorified existence otherwise than by means of the highest sensual enjoyment." (Compare pp. 443–448.)

[1] See the Author's " Origin of Nations," pp. 129, 130.

CHAPTER VII.

RELIGION OF THE ANCIENT GREEKS.

"The Greek religion was the result of the peculiar development and history of the Grecian people."—DOLLINGER, *Jew and Gentile*, vol. i. p. 68.

THAT "in general the Greek religion may be correctly described as a worship of Nature; and that most of its deities corresponded either to certain parts of the sensible world, or to certain classes of objects comprehended under abstract notions," is a remark of Bishop Thirlwall[1] in which most critics at the present day will acquiesce with readiness. Placed in a region of marked beauty and variety, and sympathising strongly with the material world around him, the lively Greek saw in the objects with which he was brought into contact, no inert mass of dull and lifeless matter, but a crowd of mighty agencies, full of a wonderful energy. The teeming earth, the quickening sun, the restless sea, the irresistible storm, every display of superhuman might which he beheld, nay, all motion and growth, impressed him with the sense of something living and working. He did not, however, like his Indian brother, deify (as a general

[1] "History of Greece," vol. i. p. 217.

176

rule) the objects themselves ; or, at any rate, if he had ever done so, it was in a remote past, of which language alone retained the trace ;[1] he did not, in the times in which he is really known to us, worship the storm, or the sun, or the earth, or the ocean, or the winds, or the rivers, but, by the power of his imagination, he invested all these things with personality. Everywhere around him, in all the different localities, and departments, and divisions, and subdivisions of the physical world, he recognised agencies of unseen beings endued with life, volition, and design. Nature was peopled for him with a countless multitude of such invisible powers, some inhabiting the earth, some the heaven, some the sea, some the dark and dreadful region beneath the earth, into which the sun's rays could not penetrate. " Of such beings," as Mr. Grote observes,[2] " there were numerous varieties, and many gradations both in power and attributes ; there were differences of age, sex, and local residence, relations, both conjugal and filial, between them, and tendencies sympathetic as well as repugnant. The gods formed a sort of political community of their own, which had its hierarchy, its distributions of ranks and duties, its contentions for power, and occasional revolutions, its public meetings in the agora of Olympus, and its multitudinous banquets or festivals. The great Olympic gods were, in fact,

[1] Zeus may have been once *Dyaus*, "the sky" (Max Muller, " Chips from a German Workshop," vol. ii. p. 72) ; but the word very early " became a proper name " and designated a person.

[2] " History of Greece," vol. i. pp. 463–465.

12

only the most exalted amongst an aggregate of quasi-human or ultra-human personages—dæmons, heroes, nymphs, eponymous genii, identified with each river, mountain, cape, town, village, or known circumscription of territory, besides horses, bulls, and dogs, of immortal breed and peculiar attributes, monsters of strange lineaments and combinations—' Gorgons, and Hydras, and Chimæras dire'—and besides 'gentile and ancestral deities,' and ' peculiar beings whose business it was to co-operate or impede in the various stages of each trade or business.'

Numerous additions might be made to this list. Not only had each mountain chain and mountain-top a separate presiding god or goddess, but troops of Oreads inhabited the mountain regions, and disported themselves among them ; not only was there a river-god to each river, a Simoïs and a Scamander, an Enipeus and an Achelous, but every nameless stream and brooklet had its water-nymph, every spring and fountain its naiad ; wood-nymphs peopled the glades and dells of the forest regions ; air-gods moved in the zephyrs and the breezes ; each individual oak had its dryad. To the gods proper were added the heroes, gods of a lower grade, and these are spoken of as "thirty thousand in number, guardian dæmons, spirits of departed heroes, who are continually walking over earth, veiled in darkness, watching the deeds of men, and dispensing weal or woe."[1]

---

[1] Thirlwall, " History of Greece," vol. i. p. 235. Compare Hesiod, " Works and Days," l. 250.

It is this multiplicity of the objects of worship, together with their lively active personality, which forms the first striking feature of the ancient Greek religion, and naturally attracts the attention of observers in the first instance. Nowhere have we such a multitudinous pantheon. Not only was the multiplicity of external nature reflected in the spiritual world as in a mirror, but every phase, and act, and circumstance of human life, every quality of the mind, every attribute of the body, might be, generally was, personified, and became a divine being. Sleep and Death, Old Age and Pain, Strength, Force, Strife, Victory, Battle, Murder, Hunger, Dreaming, Memory, Forgetfulness, Lawlessness, Law, Forethought, Afterthought, Grief, Ridicule, Retribution, Recklessness, Deceit, Wisdom, Affection, Grace, were gods or goddesses, were presented to the mind as persons, and had their place in the recognised Theogonies,[1] or systematic arrangements of the chief deities according to supposed relationship and descent. Similarly, the facts of Nature, as distinct from her parts, were personified and worshipped, Chaos, Day, Night, Time, the Hours, Dawn, Darkness, Lightning, Thunder, Echo, the Rainbow, were persons— "persons, just as much as Zeus and Apollo"[2]—though not, perhaps, so uniformly regarded in this light.

Another leading feature in the system is the existence of marked gradations of rank and power among

---

[1] Hesiod, "Theogon." ll. 114–264; Apollodorus, "Bibliotheca," i. 1–6.

[2] Grote, "History of Greece," vol. i. p. 2.

the gods, who fall into at least five definite classes,[1] clearly distinguished the one from the other. First and foremost come the Olympic deities, twelve in number, six male and six female, but not as a rule connected together in pairs—Zeus, Poseidon, Apollo, Ares, Hephæstus, Hermes, Hera, Athené, Artemis, Aphrodite, Hestia, and Demeter. Next in order are the great bulk of the gods and goddesses, Hades, Dionysus, Cronus, Uranus, Hyperion, Helios, Nereus, Proteus, Æolus, Leto, Dione, Persephone, Hecaté, Selené, Themis, Harmonia, the Graces, the Muses, the Fates, the Furies, the Eileithyiæ, the Oceanids, the Nereids, the Nymphs, the Naiads, and the like. In the third rank may be placed the deities who act as attendants on the greater gods, and perform services for them, Iris, the messenger of Jove, Hebé, his cup-bearer, Kratos and Bia, the servants of Hephæstus,[2] Boreas, Notus, etc., subordinates of Æolus, the Hours, handmaids of Aphrodite, etc. Fourthly, we may name the more shadowy gods and goddesses, Night, Day, Ether, Dawn, Darkness, Death, Sleep, Strife, Memory, Fame, Retribution, Recklessness, etc., who do not often appear as deities except in poetry, and are perhaps rather personifications consciously made than real substantive divinities. Finally must be mentioned the monstrous births ascribed to certain divine unions or marriages, *e. g.*, the Cyclopes, and Centimani, the offspring of Earth and Heaven (Gæa and Uranus); the Harpies, daughters of Thaumas

---

[1] Grote, " History of Greece," vol. i. pp. 14, 15.

[2] See .Eschyl. " Prom. Vinct." *sub init.*

and Electra, one of the Oceanidæ; the Gorgons and Grææ, children of Phorcys and Ceto; Chrysaor and Pegasus, born of the blood of Medusa, when she was slain by Perseus; Geryon and Echidna, sprung from Chrysaor and Callirrhoe; Orthros, the two-headed dog of Geryon, born of Typhaon and Echidna; Cerberus, the dog of Hades, with fifty heads; Scylla and Charybdis; the Lernæan Hydra, the Sphinx of Thebes, the Nemean Lion, the Dragon of the Hesperides, the Centaurs, the Chimæra, etc., etc.

The chief interest naturally attaches to the gods of the First Order, those commonly denominated "Olympic;" and, in a work like the present, some account must necessarily be given of the twelve deities who constituted the Olympian council.

ZEUS.

At the head of all, occupying a position quite unique and unlike that of any other, stood the great Zeus. Zeus is "*the* God, or, as he is called in later times, the Father of the gods, and the God of gods. When we ascend to the most distant heights of Greek history, the idea of God, as the Supreme Being, stands before us as a simple fact."[1] "Zeus," said an ancient poet, "is the beginning; Zeus the middle; out of Zeus have all things been made." Zeus was "the lord of the upper regions, who dwelt on the summits of the highest mountains, gathered the clouds about him, shook the air with his thunder, and wielded the lightning as the instrument of his wrath. From

[1] Max Müller, "Chips," vol. ii. p. 148.

elements drawn from these different sources his character, a strange compound of strength and weakness,
seems to have been formed by successive poets, who,
if they in some degree deserved the censure of the
philosophers, seem at least not to have been guilty of
any arbitrary fictions; while, on the other hand, by
establishing his supremacy they introduced (?) a principle of unity into the Greek polytheism, which was
not perhaps without influence on the speculations of
the philosophers themselves, though it exerted little
on the superstitions of the vulgar. The Olympian
deities are assembled round Zeus as his family, in
which he maintains the mild dignity of a patriarchal
king. He assigns their several provinces, and con-
trols their authority. Their combined efforts cannot
give the slightest shock to his power, nor retard the
execution of his will; and hence their waywardness,
even when it incurs his rebuke, cannot ruffle the inward serenity of his soul. The tremendous nod,
wherewith he confirms his decrees, can neither be re-
voked nor frustrated. As his might is irresistible,
so is his wisdom unsearchable. He holds the golden
balance in which are poised the destinies of nations
and of men; from the two vessels that stand at his
threshold he draws the good and evil gifts that alter-
nately sweeten and embitter mortal existence. The
eternal order of things, the ground of the immutable
succession of events, is his, and therefore he himself
submits to it. Human laws derive their sanction
from his ordinance; earthly kings receive their sceptre
from his hand; he is the guardian of social rights;

he watches over the fulfilment of contracts, the observance of oaths; he punishes treachery, arrogance,
and cruelty. The stranger and the suppliant are
under his peculiar protection; the fence that encloses
the family dwelling is in his keeping; he avenges
the denial and the abuse of hospitality. Yet even
this greatest and most glorious of beings, as he is
called, is subject, like the other gods, to passion and
frailty. For, though secure from dissolution, though
surpassingly beautiful and strong, and warmed with
a purer blood than fills the veins of men, their heavenly frames are not insensible to pleasure and pain;
they need the refreshment of ambrosial food, and in-
hale a grateful savour from the sacrifices of their
worshippers. Their other affections correspond to
the grossness of these animal appetites. Capricious
love and hatred, anger and jealousy, often disturb the
calm of their bosoms; the peace of the Olympian state
might be broken by factions, and even by conspiracies
formed against its chief. He himself cannot keep
perfectly aloof from their quarrels; he occasionally
wavers in his purpose, is overruled by artifice, blinded
by desires, and hurried by resentment into unseemly
violence. The relation in which he stands to Fate is
not uniformly represented in the Homeric poems, and
probably the poet had not formed a distinct notion
of it. Fate is generally described as emanating from
his will, but sometimes he appears to be no more than
the minister of a stern necessity, which he wishes in
vain to elude."[1]

[1] Thirlwall, "History of Greece," vol. i. pp. 217–219.

And Zeus bears to man the relation of "father." Each mortal who has a supplication to make to him, may address him as Ζευ πά-ερ, "God (our) Father." He bears, as one of his most usual titles, the designation of "Father of gods and men." As St. Paul says,[1] quoting a Greek poet, "we are his offspring." The entire passage where these words occur is remarkable, and very instructive on the Grecian idea of Zeus.

> " With Zeus begin we—let no mortal voice
>   Leave Zeus unpraised. Zeus fills the haunts of men,
>   The streets, the marts—Zeus fills the sea, the shores,
>   The harbours—everywhere we live in Zeus.
>   We are his offspring too; friendly to man,
>   He gives prognostics ; sets men to their toil
>   By need of daily bread : tells when the land
>   Must be upturned by ploughshare or by spade—
>   What time to plant the olive or the vine—
>   What time to fling on earth the golden grain.
>   For He it was who scattered o'er the sky
>   The shining stars, and fixed them where they are—
>   Provided constellations through the year.
>   To mark the seasons in their changeless course.
>   Wherefore men worship Him—the First—the Last—
>   Their Father—Wonderful—their Help and Shield." [2]

A pantheistic tinge pervades this description ; but still in parts it approaches to some of the most beautiful and sublime expressions of Holy Writ.[3]   It

[1] Acts xvii. 28.

[2] Aratus, "Phænomena," ll. 1–15.

[3] Compare "everywhere we live in Zeus" with "in Him we live, and move, and have our being" (Acts xvii. 28)—the provision of constellations with Gen. i. 14—the term "Wonderful" with Isa. ix. 6—"the First, the Last" with Rev. i. 8, 11, etc."— "their Help and Shield" with Psa. xviii. 2; xlvi. 1, etc.

presents Zeus to us as omnipresent, beneficent, worthy of perpetual praise, our father, our help and defence, our support and stay. It sets him forth as "wonderful," or rather "a mighty wonder"—μέγα θαυμα—a being beyond our power to comprehend, whom we must be content to reverence and admire. It recognises him as having hung the stars in the blue vault of heaven, and having set them there "for signs, and for seasons, and for days, and years." It calls him "the First" and "the Last"—the Alpha and the Omega of being.

Such is the strength of Zeus, according to the Greek idea; but withal there is a weakness about him, which sinks him, not only below the "Almighty" of Scripture, but even below the Ormazd of the Persians. He has a material frame, albeit of an ethereal and subtle fibre; and requires material sustenance. According to some of the myths, he was born in time; according to all, he was once a god of small power. Heaven had its revolutions in the Greek system: and as the sovereignty of Olympus had passed from Uranus to Cronus, and from Cronus to Zeus in former times, so in the future it might pass, and according to some, was doomed to pass, from Zeus to another.[1] Nor was he without moral defect. A rebellious son, a faithless husband, not always a kind father, he presented to the moral consciousness no perfect pattern for man's imitation, but a strange and monstrous combination of wicked-

---

[1] Æschyl. "Prom. Vinct." ll. 939-959.

ness with high qualities, of weakness with strength, of good with evil.[1]

POSEIDON.

Poseidon is reckoned as the second of the Olympic gods, rather as being, in the mythology, the brother of Zeus, than from any superiority of his own over the rest of the Olympians.[2]   He is viewed as especially the god of the sea, and is worshipped chiefly by maritime states and in cities situated on or near the coast; but he has also a considerable hold upon the land, and is "earth-shaking" and "earth-possessing," quite as decidedly as sovereign ruler of the seas and ocean.   His worship is ancient, and in many places has given way to an introduction of later and more fashionable deities.   It has traces of a rudeness and roughness that are archaic, and stands connected with the more grotesque and barbarous element in the religion.   "Among his companions are wild Titans and spiteful dæmons,"[3] human sacrifices are offered to him; horses are buried alive in his honour; Polyphemus the Cyclops, whom Ulysses punishes, is his son; and his offspring generally are noted for huge size and great corporeal strength.[4]   It has been maintained that his cult was of foreign origin, having been introduced among the Greeks by the

[1] Compare Mr. Gladstone's remarks in his "Homer and the Homeric Age," vol. ii. pp. 186–190.

[2] Poseidon claims in the "Iliad" an authority within his own domain independent of Zeus ("Iliad," xv. 174 *et seqq.*), but exercises no right of rule over any other god.

[3] Curtius, "History of Greece," vol. i. p. 56.

[4] Hom. "Odyssey," xi. 505–520.

Carians,[1] or by the Libyans;[2] but there are no sufficient grounds for these refinements, or for separating off Poseidon from the bulk of the Olympic deities, admittedly of native growth, and having a general family resemblance. If Poseidon is cast in a
ruder and rougher mould than most of the others,
we may account for it by the character of his element, and the boisterousness of sailors, who were at
all times his principal worshippers. Poseidon's
roughness is compensated for by a solidity and
strength of character, not too common among the
Grecian deities; he is not readily turned from his
purpose; blandishments have little effect upon him;
failure does not discourage him; he is persistent,
and generally, though not always, successful. His
hostility to Troy, arising from his treatment by Lao-
medon, conduced greatly towards that city's destruction; and the offence which he took at the decision
of Erechtheus led to the final overthrow of that
hero's family. On the other hand, his persecution
of Ulysses, on account of the chastisement which he
had inflicted on Polyphemus, does not prevent the
final return of that much-enduring wanderer to
Ithaca, nor does his opposition succeed in hindering
the settlement of Æneas, with his Trojan companions,
in Latium. For grandeur and sublimity of character
and position Poseidon cannot compare with Zeus, whom

---

[1] Curtius, vol. i. p. 298: "The Carians introduced [into Greece]
the worship of the Carian Zeus, and of Poseidon."

[2] Herod. ii. 50: iv. 188.

however, he sometimes ventures to beard;[1] in respect of moral conduct he is in no way Zeus's superior; in respect of intellectual elevation he falls decidedly below him.

APOLLO.

The conception of Apollo as the sun is a late form of Hellenic belief, and must be wholly put aside when we are considering the religion of the *ancient* Greeks. Apollo seems to have been originally, like Zeus, a representation of the one God, originating probably in some part of Greece where Zeus was unknown,[2] and subsequently adopted into the system prevalent in Homeric times, and in this system subordinated to Zeus as his son and interpreter. Compared with Zeus, he is a spiritualised conception. Zeus is the embodiment of creative energy and almighty power: Apollo of divine prescience, of healing skill, and of musical and poetic production. "In Apollo Hellenic polytheism received its harmonious completion, and the loftiest glorification of which it was capable."[3]

Apollo rises on the vision of one familiar with Greek antiquity as almost a pure conception, almost an angelic divinity. To a form of ideal beauty, combining youthful grace and vigour with the fullest perfection of manly strength, he added unerring wisdom, complete insight into futurity, an un-

---

[1] Hom. "Iliad," xv. 175.

[2] Curtius suggests Lycia or Crete ("History of Greece," vol. i. p. 59).

[3] *Ibid.*

stained life, ¹ the magic power of song, ability and
will to save and heal, together with the dread prero-
gative of dealing out at his pleasure destruction and
death. Compassionate on occasions as Mercy herself,
he shows at times the keen and awful severity of a
destroying archangel. *Ekebolos,* " striking from
afar," he speeds his fatal shafts from his unfailing
bow, and smites whomsoever he will with a death-
stroke which there is no escaping. Never offended
without cause, never moved by caprice, he works the
will of Zeus in all that he does, dispenses retributive
justice, and purifies with wholesome fear the souls of
men. Partaker of all the counsels of his father, and
permitted to use his discretion in communicating
them to the denizens of earth, he delivers his oracular
responses from the various spots which he has chosen
as his special abodes, and, though sometimes his
replies may be of doubtful import, seldom sends
away a votary unsatisfied. The answers which he
gives, or at any rate is supposed to give, determine
the decisions of statesmen,² and shape the course of
history. War and peace, treaties and alliances, are
made and unmade, as the Delphic and other oracles
inspired by him advise; and the course of Hellenic
colonisation is almost entirely determined by his
decrees.³

Poet, prophet, physician, harper, god of victory

¹ See this point discussed in **Mr. Gladstone's** " Homer and the
Homeric Age," (vol. ii. pp. 106–111).

² Herod. vii. 140–143.

³ *Ibid.* iv. 150–159; v. 42, etc.

and angel of death in one, Apollo is always on the side of right, always true to Zeus, and not much inferior to him in power. It is, perhaps, a fanciful analogy which has been traced between him and the Second Person of the Christian Trinity;[1] but the very fact that such an analogy can be suggested is indicative of the pure and lofty character of the god, which equals at any rate, if it does not transcend, the highest ideal of divinity that has hitherto been elaborated by unassisted human wisdom.

ARES.

It has been well said that Ares is "the impersonation of a passion." That combative propensity, which man possesses in common with a large number of animals, was regarded by the Greeks, not only as a divine thing, but as a thing of such lofty divinity

[1] Friedriech says: "This triad of Zeus, Athené, and Apollo bears an unmistakeable analogy to the Christian Trinity of Father, Son, and Holy Ghost: Zeus answering to God the Father, Athene to the Holy Ghost, and *Apollo to the Son of God, the Declarer of the will of his Heavenly Father*" ("Die Realien in der Iliade und Odyssee," part iii. pp. 635 and 689). Mr. Gladstone came independently to the same conclusion, and says:—"In Apollo are represented the legendary anticipations of a person to come, in whom should be combined all the great offices in which God the Son is now made known to man, as the Light of our paths, the Physician of our diseases, the Judge of our misdeeds, and the Conqueror and Disarmer, but not yet Abolisher, of death," ("Homer and the Homeric Age," vol. ii. p. 132). Professor Max Müller, on the other hand, thinks that "it seems blasphemy to consider the fables of the heathen world as corrupted and misinterpreted fragments of a divine revelation once granted to the whole of mankind" ("Chips from a German Workshop," vol. ii. p. 13).

that its representative must have a place among the deities of the first class or order. The propensity itself was viewed as common to man with the gods, and as having led to "wars in heaven," wherein all the greater deities had borne their part. Now that peace was established in the Olympian abode, it found a vent on earth, and caused the participation of the gods in the wars carried on among mortals. Ares was made the son of Zeus and Hera, the king and queen of heaven. He was represented as tall, handsome, and active, but as cruel, lawless, and greedy of blood. The finer elements of the warlike spirit are not his. He is a divine Ajax,[1] rather than a divine Achilles; and the position which he occupies in the Olympian circle is low. Apollo and Athene are both entitled to give him their orders; and Athene scolds him, strikes him senseless, and wounds him through the spear of Diomed.[2] His worship is thought to have been derived from Thrace,[3] and to have been introduced into Greece only a little before the time of Homer.[4] It was at no time very widely spread, or much affected by any Grecian tribe or state, the conception being altogether too coarse to attract the sympathies of a refined people.

[1] Mr. Gladstone says, "not so much an Ajax as a Caliban" ("Homer and the Homeric Age," vol. ii. p. 228); but is not this too harsh a view, even of the Homeric conception of Ares?

[2] Hom. "Iliad," v. 885–887; xv. 110–142, etc.

[3] Döllinger, Jew and Gentile," vol. i. p. 88.

[4] Gladstone, "Homer and the Homeric Age," vol. ii. pp. 229–231.

HEPHÆSTUS.

Hephæstus is the god of fire, and especially of fire in connection with smelting and metallurgy. He dwells in Lemnos, where he habitually forges thunderbolts for Zeus, and occasionally produces fabrics in metal of elaborate and exquisite construction. Among the most marvellous of his works are the automatic tripods of Olympus and the bronze maidens, whom he has formed to be his attendants on account of his lameness. He is the armourer of heaven, and provides the gods generally with the weapons which they use in warfare. The peculiarity of his lameness is strange and abnormal, since the Greeks hate deformity, and represent their deities generally as possessed of perfect physical beauty. It has been accounted for on the supposition that he is a Grecised Phthah,[1] introduced from Egypt, directly or indirectly,[2] and that his deformity is a modification of Phthah's presentment as a pigmy with the lower limbs misshapen. But the features common to Hephæstus with Phthah are few; the name of Hephæstus is probably of pure Greek etymology, connected with φάος and φαίνω; and, on the whole, there would seem to be no evidence that Hephæstus is a foreign god more than any other. Rather, it is characteristic of the many sidedness of the Greeks,

---

[1] Sir G. Wilkinson in Rawlinson's " Herodotus," vol. ii., p. 139, note (3rd edition).

[2] Mr. Gladstone regards him as introduced from Phœnicia (" Homer and the Homeric Age," vol. ii. p. 255).

and consequent upon the anthropomorphism which makes the Olympic community a reflection of earthly things, that there should be even in this august conclave something provocative of laughter, a discord to break the monotony of the harmony, an element of grotesqueness and monstrosity. Hephæstus in the Olympic halls is like the jester at the court of a mediæval monarch, a something to lighten the seriousness of existence, to provoke occasionally a burst of that "inextinguishable laughter," without which life in so sublime an atmosphere would be intolerable. The marriage of Hephæstus to Aphrodite is conceived in the same spirit. There was a keen sense of humour in the countrymen of Aristophanes; and the combination of the clumsy, lame, and begrimed smith with the Queen of Beauty and Love pleased their sense of the ludicrous, and was the fertile source of many an amusing legend. "The Lay of the Net," wherewith Demodocus entertains both gods and men,[1] is a sufficient specimen of this class of lively myth, and shows that the comic features of ill-assorted marriage, on which modern playwrights have traded so freely, were fully appreciated by the Greeks, and were supposed well-suited to provoke the gods to merriment. The modern moralist will regret this unworthy representation of divine beings;[2] but it is quite in accord with the general character of the Greek religion, which reflected back upon deity all that was weak, as well as all that was strong, in man.

---

[1] Hom. "Odyss." viii. 266–366.

[2] "Homer and the Homeric Age," vol. ii. pp. 461–463.

HERMES.

Hermes is the impersonation of commercial dealings, and hence a god who gives wealth and increase, a god of inventive power, and a god of tricks and thievery. He is "the Olympian man of business,"[1] and therefore employed in embassies and commissions, and even sometimes in the simple carrying of messages. As δώτωρ εἀων,[2] "the giver of comforts," he secures his votaries all manner of worldly prosperity. He is industrious and inventive, constructs the seven-stringed lyre before he is a day old,[3] afterwards invents the pan's-pipes, and ultimately becomes a god of wisdom and learning generally. His thievishness must be taken to show that commercial fraud is pretty well as ancient as commerce itself, and that "the good old times" were not, as sometimes represented, an age of innocence. It has been said that he is more human than any other Olympian god ; and that "he represents, so to speak, the utilitarian side of the human mind,"[4] being active, energetic, fruitful in resource, a keen bargainer, a bold story-teller, and a clever thief. His admission into the number of the Olympians is the strongest possible indication of the inferiority of the moral standard among the Greeks. The special regard paid to him by the Athenians is, however, perhaps the

[1] Dollinger, "Jew and Gentile, vol. i. p. 74.
[2] Hom. "Odyss. viii. 335. Compare "Iliad," xiv. 490.
[3] Hom. "Hym. Merc." l. 16.
[4] "Homer and the Homeric Age," vol. ii. p. 242.

mere consequence of their addiction to the pursuits of commerce.

Hermes is commonly represented as a youth just attaining to manhood. The wings which adorn his head and ankles indicate the celerity of his movements. His caduceus is perhaps the golden rod of wealth given to him by Apollo in exchange for the lyre. It represents also the staff commonly borne by heralds, and in this point of view had white ribands attached to it, which in later times became serpents. Sometimes he holds a purse in his hand, to mark his power of bestowing riches.

The six female Olympic deities—Hera, Athene, Artemis, Aphrodité, Hestia, and Demeter—have now to be considered.

HERA.

The anthropomorphism which was so main an element in the Greek religion made it requisite that motherhood, as well as fatherhood, should be enthroned in the Olympic sphere, that Zeus should have his consort, heaven its queen, and women their representative in the highest celestial position. Hera was, perhaps, originally Era, " the Earth ;"[1] but this idea was soon lost sight of, and in Greek mythology, from first to last, she is quite other than the principle of mundane fecundity, quite a different being from the oriental earth-goddess, called indifferently Cybele,

[1] See Mr. Gladstone's " Homer and the Homeric Age," vol. ii. p. 190. Others suggest a connection with *heros, herus, hera,* and so with the German *herr,* and our *sir.*

Dindymené, Magna Mater, Rhea, Beltis, Mylitta, etc.
Hera is, primarily, the wife of Zeus, the queen of
the Olympic court, the mistress of heaven. She is
"a reflected image of Zeus,"[1] and exercises all her
husband's prerogatives, thunders, shakes Olympus,
makes Iris her messenger, gives her orders to the
Winds and the Sun, confers valour, and the like.
As the personification of maternity, she presides over
child-birth; and the Eileithyiæ, her daughters, act as
her ministers. She does not present to us an elevated
idea of female perfection, since, despite her exalted
rank, she is subject to numerous feminine infirmities.
Mr. Grote notes that she is "proud, jealous, and
bitter."[2] Mr. Gladstone observes that she is pas-
sionate, wanting in moral elevation, cruel, vindictive,
and unscrupulous.[3] Her mythological presentation
was certainly not of a nature to improve the character
of those women who might take her for their model;
since, although she was possessed of certain great
qualities, passion, fervour, strong affection, self-com-
mand, courage, acuteness, yet she was, on the whole,
wanting in the main elements of female excellence,
gentleness, softness, tenderness, patience, submission
to wrong, self renunciation, reticence. She was a
proud, grand, haughty, powerful queen; not a kind,
helpful, persuasive, loving woman. The mythology
of Greece is in few points less satisfactory than in the

[1] "Homer and the Homeric Age," vol. ii. p. 194.

[2] "History of Greece," vol. i. p. 50.

[3] "Homer and the Homeric Age," vol. ii. pp. 190–196.

type of female character which it exhibits at the head of its pantheon.

ATHENÉ.

If Hera is below the level of female excellence which we might have expected refined heathens to have represented in a chief goddess, Athene is above the level. She has a character which is without a flaw. Originally, as it would seem, a conscious impersonation of the divine wisdom, and therefore fabled to have sprung full-grown from the head of Zeus, she became a distinct and substantive deity at a very early date, and was recognised as the "goddess of wisdom, war, polity, and industrial art."[1] Homer places her, together with Zeus and Apollo, on a higher platform of divinity than the other deities,[2] and makes her even oppose Zeus when he is in the wrong, thwart him, and vindicate right and truth in his despite.[3] It has been said that she is "without feminine sympathies—the type of composed, majestic, and unrelenting force;"[4] and this is so far true that she has certainly little softness, absolutely no weakness, and not many distinctly feminine characteristics. But she was recognised, like her Egyptian counterpart, Neith, as the goddess of good housewifery, "patronising handicraft, and expert at

[1] "Homer and the Homeric Age," vol. ii. p. 59.

[2] Hom. "Iliad," ii. 371; iv. 288; vii. 132, etc.; "Odyss." iv. 341; xvii. 132, etc.

[3] "Iliad," viii. 30–40,

[4] Grote, "History of Greece," vol. i. p. 47.

the loom and spindle,"[1] no less than as the wise directress of statesmen and warriors. Undoubtedly, the atmosphere in which she removed was too cold, calm, and clear for her ever to have attached to herself any very large share of human sympathy; but she exercised an elevating influence on the nobler spirits of both sexes, as combining the three attributes of purity, strength, and wisdom in the highest possible degree, and so furnishing at once a model for imitation, and a support and stay for feeble souls in the spirit world, where they had otherwise little on which they could place any firm reliance. The universally-received myth of Mentor and Telemachus acted as a strong reinforcement to the power of conscience, which the young Greek felt might be the voice of Athene speaking within him, advising him for his true good, and pointing out to him the path of honour and duty. Athene's special connection with Athens and Attica added much to her importance in the Greek religious system, since it brought the best minds and most generous natures of Hellas peculiarly under the influence of a thoroughly high and noble religious conception.

ARTEMIS.

Artemis is altogether a shadowy divinity. She is a "pale reflection of her brother,"[2] Phœbus Apollo, whose attributes she reproduces in a subdued form, being, like him, majestic, pure, chaste, a minis-

---

[1] Grote, "History of Greece," vol. p. 47.
[2] "Homer and the Homeric Age," vol. ii. p. 143.

ter of death, and a dexterous archer. Nothing is peculiar to her except her presidency over hunting, which determined her general presentation to the eye by the Greek artists. She embodied and personified that passion for the chase which was common to the Hellenes with most energetic races. It was supposed that she dwelt mainly upon earth, haunting the forests and the mountains, dressed as a huntress, and accompanied by her favorite hounds. Her connection with the moon was an after-thought in the Greek mythology, as was that of Apollo with the sun. It arose mainly from the fact that hunters, to be successful, had to commence their operations by night, and needed the light of the moon in order to make their arrangements.

The Artemis of Ephesus was the embodiment of a different idea.[1] She took the place of the great Asiatic Nature-goddess—Cybele, Rhea, Magna Mater, Beltis, Mylitta—and had nothing in common with the Artemis of Hellas proper but the name. "Her image, shaped like a mummy, was of black wood; the upper part of the body was ornamented with the breasts of animals, the lower with figures of them."[2] She was a mere impersonation of the principle of fecundity in nature—"a Pantheistic deity, with more of an Asiatic than Hellenic character."[3]

APHRODITÉ.

Aphrodite is the antithesis, and in some sort the complement, of Athene. She is the impersonation of

---

[1] Grote, "History of Greece," vol. i. p. 48.

[2] Döllinger, "Jew and Gentile," vol. i. p. 86. [3] *Ibid.*

all that is soft and weak and erring in female nature, as Athene is of all that is high and pure and strong. Goddess of beauty and love, not, however, of love in its more elevated form, but rather of sensual desire, she was received by the Greeks probably from an Asiatic source, but so transmuted and Hellenised as to have become, when we first meet with her, a completely national divinity.[1] Hellenic in the whole character of her beauty, she is well described by a living English poet[2] in a passage which is eminently classical:—

> " Idalian Aphrodite beautiful,
>   Fresh as the foam, new bathed in Paphian wells,
>   With rosy slender fingers backward drew
>   From her warm brow and bosom her deep hair
>   Ambrosial, golden round her lucid throat
>   And shoulder: from the violets her light foot
>   Shone rosy white, and o'er her rounded form,
>   Between the shadows of the vine-branches,
>   Floated the golden sunlight as she moved."

Nothing so lovely in form and colour and texture and combination of rare charms, graced the splendid chambers of the Olympian court—nothing so ravishing had ever presented itself to the vision of painter or poet. But the beauty was altogether physical, sensuous, divorced alike from moral goodness and

[1] Mr. Gladstone takes a different view. He regards the Aphrodite of Homer as scarcely a Greek divinity (" Homer and the Homeric Age," vol. ii. pp. 244, 245). But to me it seems that, even in Homer, her character is as thoroughly Greek as her name.

[2] See Tennyson's " Œnone," ll. 170-178.

mental power. Silly and childish, easily tricked and imposed upon, Aphrodite is mentally contemptible, while morally she is odious. Tyrannical over the weak, cowardly before the strong, frail herself, and the persistent stirrer up of frailty in others, lazy, deceitful, treacherous, selfish, shrinking from the least touch of pain, she repels the moral sentiment with a force almost equal to that wherewith she attracts the lower animal nature. Hence the Greek cannot speak of her without the most violent conflict of feeling. He is drawn to her, but he detests her; he is fascinated, yet revolted; he admires, yet he despises and condemns; and his condemnation, on the whole, outweighs his admiration. He calls her

> "A goddess verily of many names—
> Not Cypris only, but dark Hades, too,
> And Force resistless, and mad, frantic Rage,
> And sheer untempered Craving, and shrill Grief." [1]

He allows, but he rebels against her power over him; he protests even when he surrenders himself; and hence, on the whole, Aphrodite exercises a less corrupting influence in Greece than might have been anticipated. That the pantheon should contain a goddess of the kind was of course to some extent debasing. Bad men could justify themselves by the divine example, and plead powerlessness to resist a divine impulse. But their conscience was not satisfied; they felt they sinned against their higher nature; and thus, after all, the moral standard was

[1] Sophocl. Fragm. xxiii. (ed. Brunck).

not very seriously affected by the existence of the Cyprian goddess among the Olympic deities.

HESTIA.

Hestia is still more shadowy than Artemis. She is, in part, the femine counterpart of Hephæstus, the goddess of fire ; but she is principally the impersonation of the sacred character of each hearth and home, whether domestic, tribal, or national. Hestia presided over the private hearths and homesteads of all Greeks, over the Prytaneia of cities, and over the altars kept ablaze in the temples which were centres of confederacies. She invested them with a sacred character, watched over them, protected them. Her personality was but slightly developed. Still she seems to have been regarded as possessing, to a remarkable extent, the qualities of holiness and purity ; and thus to have practically maintained in Greek domestic life a high and pure standard, such as has scarcely been much exceeded among Christians. She was fabled to have vowed perpetual virginity ; and it is clear that, together with Athene and Artemis, she upheld among the Greeks the idea of virginal purity as a transcendental phase of life, a moral perfection whereto the best and purest might not only aspire, but attain, as the result of earnest endeavour.

DEMETER.

Demeter, the "Earth-Mother," was an original Greek conception, corresponding to one common among the Oriental nations, the conception personi-

fied by Maut in Egypt, Beltis or Mylitta in Babylon,
Cybele in Phrygia, etc. The earth on which man
lives, and from which he derives the food that sustains him, was viewed as a kind and bountiful parent
—the nurse, the feeder, the supporter, the sustainer
of mankind. Personified as a goddess, she demanded
the worship and gratitude of all, and was hence a
universal deity, though specially honoured in certain
places. In the Greek religion Demeter was closely
connected with agriculture, since the earth in Greece
did not support men without toil. She made the
Greeks acquainted with the growing of cereals, the
operations of tillage, and bread-making. Moreover,
as agriculture was "the foundation of all social and
political ordinances, and inseparably connected with
the introduction of peaceable and orderly ways of
life, Demeter, under her title of Thesmophoros, was
the ennobler of mankind, the founder of civilisation
and lawgiving." She was thus more in Greece than
she was in Asia. Her position in the greatest of the
mysteries—the Eleusinian—was probably owing to
this double function, this combination of a Nature-
goddess with a deity of law and order, the power
that led man on from the simple nomadic condition
to all the refinements and complications of advanced
political life.

"These were the prime in order and in might;
The rest were long to tell, though far renown'd,
Th' Ionian gods, of Javan's issue held
Gods, yet confess'd later than heav'n and earth,
Their boasted parents: Titan, Heav'n's first-born,
With his enormous brood, and birthright seiz'd

By younger Saturn : he from mightier Jove,
His own and Reah's son, like measure found :
So Jove usurping reign'd : these first in Crete
And Ida known ; thence on the snowy top
Of cold Olympus rul'd the middle air,
Their highest heav'n ; or on the Delphian cliff,
Or in Dodona, and through all the bounds
Of Doric land ; or who with Saturn old
Fled over Adria to th' Hesperian fields,
And o'er the Celtic roam'd the utmost isles.

* * * * * *

Nor had they yet among the sons of Eve
Got them new names ; till wand'ring o'er the earth,
Through God's high suff'rance for the trial of man,
By falsities and lies the greatest part
Of mankind they corrupted to forsake
God their Creator, and th' invisible
Glory of Him that made them to transform
Oft to the image of a brute, adorn'd
With gay religions full of pomp and gold,
And devils to adore for deities :
Then they were known to men by various names,
And various idols through the heathen world."—

Among the deities external to the Olympic circle, the most important were Dionysus, Leto, Persephone, and Hades or Aidoneus. Dionysus is generally admitted to have been derived from an Oriental source. The word probably meant originally "the judge of men," [1] and referred to a special function of the god, who was thought to pass sentence on the departed when they reached the other world.

Essentially, however, Dionysus was the god of inebriety, the deification of drunkenness, as Ares

[1] See the "Transactions, of the Society of Biblical Archæology," vol. ii. pp. 33, 34.

was of violence, and Aphrodite of sensual desire. He was viewed as the creator of the vine, or at any rate as its introducer into Greece; the teacher of its culture, and the discoverer of the exhilarating properties of its fruit. The worship of Dionysus was effected by taking part in his orgies, and these were of a furious and ecstatic character, accompanied with exciting music, with wild dances, with shrieks and cries, and sometimes with bloodshed. Both men and women joined in the Dionysiac rites, the women outdoing the men in the violence of their frenzy. "Crowds of females, clothed with fawn-skins, and bearing the sacred thyrsus, flocked to the solitudes of Parnassus or Cithæron or Taygetus, during the consecrated triennial period, passed the night there with torches, and abandoned themselves to demonstrations of frantic excitement, with dancing and clamorous invocation of the god. The men yielded to a similar impulse by noisy revels in the streets, sounding the cymbals and tambourine, and carrying the image of the god in procession."[1] Every sort of license and excess was regarded as lawful on these occasions, and the worship of the deity was incomplete unless the votary reached an advanced stage of intoxication. Dionysiac festivals were fortunately not of frequent recurrence, and were not everywhere celebrated in the same way. At Athens women took no part in the Dionysia; and with men intellectual contests, and the witnessing of them, held the place of the rude revels elsewhere too common. Still the influence of

[1] Grote, "History of Greece," vol. i. p. 26.

Dionysiac worship on Greece generally must be regarded as excessively corrupting, and Dionysus must be viewed as, next to Aphrodite, the most objectionable of the Greek divinities.

Leto, or Latona, as the Romans called her, when they adopted her into their pantheon, was, on the contrary, one of the purer and more elevating influences. She is wife of Zeus by a title quite as good as that of Hera,[1] and is a model of motherly love and wifely purity. Separate and peculiar function she has none, and it is difficult to account for her introduction among the Olympians. Perhaps she is to be regarded as ideal womanhood. Silent, unobtrusive, always subordinating herself to her children, majestic, chaste, kindly, ready to help and tend, she is in Olympus what the Greek wished his wife to be in his own home, her very shadowiness according with the Greek notion of womanly perfection.[2] Mr. Gladstone suggests that she is a traditional deity, representing the woman through whom man's redemption was to come;[3] but there scarcely seems sufficient foundation for this view, which is not supported by any analogies in the mythologies of other nations.

Persephone, the Roman Proserpine, was the queen of the dead; far more than her shadowy husband, Hades, the real ruler of the infernal realm. She

[1] Hesiod says that she became the wife of Zeus before Hera ("Theogony," ll. 918–221).

[2] Compare the line of Sophocles—

"O woman, silence is the woman's crown."

(*Ajax*, I. 293.)

[3] "Homer and the Homeric Age," vol. ii. p. 153.

was represented as severely pure and chaste, even having become a wife against her will, and as awful and terrible, but not cruel. She occupied no very important post in the religion, since her sphere was wholly the nether world, which only very slightly engaged the attention of the Hellenes. Hades, or Aidoneus, had a high rank, as the brother of Zeus, and in some sort his co-equal; but he was as shadowy as the realm over which he presided, and to most Greeks was simply *magni nominis umbra*— "the shadow of a great name," which they must reverence when they heard it, but not a deity who to any extent occupied their thoughts, or received their worship.[1]

It would be easy to occupy many more pages with the Greek minor deities, but our limits compel us to refrain, and to turn at this point from the objects to the character of the worship, and to the real practical influence of their religion upon the Greek race.

In the main, the Greek worship was of a joyous, pleasant, and lightsome kind. The typical Greek was devoid of any deep sense of sin—thought well of himself—did not think very highly of the gods, and considered that, so long as he kept free from grave and heinous offences, either against the moral law or against the *amour-propre* of the deities, he had little to fear, while he had much to hope, from

[1] Compare Dollinger, "Jew and Gentile," vol. i. p. 93: "The people did not trouble themselves much about Hades, and they saw no altars dedicated to him. There was one image of him at Athens, but he had hardly anywhere a regular worship."

them.   He prayed and offered sacrifice, not so much
in the way of expiation, or to deprecate God's wrath,
as in the way of natural piety, to ask for blessings
and to acknowledge them.   He made vows to the
gods in sickness, danger, or difficulty, and was careful to perform his vow on escape or recovery.   His
house was full of shrines, on which he continually
laid small offerings, to secure the favour and protection of his special patron deities.   Plato says that he
prayed every morning and evening, and also concluded every set meal with a prayer or hymn.   But
these devotions seem not to have been very earnest
or deep, and were commonly hurried through in a
perfunctory manner.

Practically, the religious worship of the Greeks
consisted mainly in attendance on festivals which
might be Pan-Hellenic, political, tribal, or peculiar
to a guild or a *phratria.*   Each year brought round
either one or two of the great panegyries—the festivals of the entire Greek race at Olympia and Delphi,
at Nemea and the Isthmus of Corinth.   There were
two great Ionic festivals annually, one at Delos, and
the other at the Panionium near Mycale.   Each state
and city throughout Greece had its own special
festivals, Dionysia, Eleusinia, Panathenæa, Carneia,
Hyakinthia, Apaturia, etc.   Most of these were
annual, and some lasted several days.   A Greek had
no "Sunday"—no sacred day recurring at set inter-
vals, on which his thoughts were bound to be
directed to religion; but so long a time as a week
scarcely ever passed without his calendar calling him

to some sacred observance or other, some feast or ceremony, in honour of some god or goddess, or in commemoration of some event important in the history of mankind,[1] or in that of his race, or of his city. And these festivals were highly attractive to him. Generally they were joyful occasions from first to last, celebrated with music, and processions, with gymnastic or orchestral competitions, or with theatrical contests. Ordinarily they include sacrifice, and feasting upon the victims sacrificed. Even when they were professedly of a mournful character, like the Spartan Hyakinthia, the opening days of which were days of sadness and of gloom, they commonly concluded with a more genial time—a time of banqueting and dancing. Accordingly, the Greek looked forward to his holy days as true holidays, and was pleased to combine duty with pleasure by taking his place in the procession, or the temple, or the theatre, to which inclination and religion alike called him. Thousands and tens of thousands flocked to each of the great Pan-Hellenic gatherings, delighting in the splendour and excitement of the scene, in the gay dresses, the magnificent equipages, the races, the games, the choric, and other contests. " These festivals," as has been well observed,[2] " were considered as the very cream of the Greek life, their periodical recurrence being expected with eagerness and greeted

---

[1] *E. g.,* the Hydrophoria, kept in commemoration of those who perished in the Flood of Deucalion, the Greek representation of the Noachical Deluge.

[2] Dollinger, " Jew and Gentile," vol. i. p. 238.

14

with joy." Similarly, though to a minor extent, each national or even tribal gathering was an occasion of enjoyment; cheerfulness, hilarity, sometimes an excessive exhilaration, prevailed; and the religion of the Greeks, in these its most striking and obvious manifestations, was altogether bright, festive, and pleasurable.

But, just as sunshine cannot exist without shadow, so even the Greek religion, bright as it was, had its dark side. Calamities befel nations, families, or individuals, and were attributed to an offended god or a cruel fury. A sense of guilt occasionally visited those who had committed great and flagrant crimes, as perjury, blasphemy, robbery of temples, incest, violation of the right of asylum, treachery toward a guest-friend, and the like. A load under these circumstances lay upon the conscience; all the horrors of remorse were felt; avenging fiends were believed to haunt and torture the guilty one, who sometimes earnestly sought relief for a term of years, and sought in vain. There were, indeed, rites of expiation appropriate to different occasions; most sins could be atoned for in some manner or other; but the process was generally long and painful;[1] and there were cases where the persistent anger of the fierce Erinyes could not in any way be appeased. When a nation had sinned, human sacrifices were not unfrequently prescribed as the only possible propitia-

[1] See the " Eumenides " of Æschylus, where Orestes, however, is at last purged of his guilt.

tion ;[1] if the case were that of an individual, various modes of purification were adopted, ablutions, fastings, sacrifices, and the like. According to Plato, however, the number of those who had any deep sense of their guilt was few: most men, whatever crimes they committed, found among the gods examples of similar acts,[2] and thought no great blame would attach to them for their misconduct. At the worst, if the gods were angered by their behaviour, a few offerings would satisfy them, and set things straight,[3] leaving the offenders free to repeat their crimes, and so to grow more and more hardened in iniquity.

At the position which the " mysteries" occupied in the Greek religion it is impossible for us, in this slight sketch, to do more than glance. The mysteries were certain secret rites practised by voluntary associations of individuals, who pledged themselves not to reveal to the uninitiated anything which they saw or heard at the secret meetings. They were usually connected with the worship of some particular god, and consisted mainly in symbolical representations of the adventures and circumstances connected with the god in the mythology. They contained nothing that was contradictory to the popular religion, and little that was explanatory of it. The various mysteries had each its own apparatus of

[1] Even as late as the time of Solon, Epimenides prescribed a human sacrifice at Athens.

[2] Plato, " Republic," ii. § 17.

[3] *Ibid.* § 7.

symbols and formularies, by which the *mystæ* knew each other, as freemasons do; but they only vaguely hinted at any theological dogmas or opinions. The Greek greatly affected these secret rites; and it is said that but few Greeks were not initiated in some mystery or other.[1] "Their attraction lay in their veil of secrecy, transparent though it was, in the variety of feelings brought into play by lively dramatic representations, in the rapid transition from anxiety and suspense to serenity and joy, the combination of all arts and artistic enjoyments, of music and song, the mimic dance, the brilliant lighting-up, and effective decoration."[2] It can scarcely, however, be said that the mysteries exercised any salutary or elevating influence on the Greeks generally. The moral conduct of the initiated was no better than that of others; and Plato thought that participation in the Eleusinia served only to strengthen and make a man secure in unrighteousness.[3]

[1] Dollinger, "Jew and Gentile," vol. i. p 193.
[2] *Ibid.* p. 196.
[3] "Republic," ii. § 6 (quoted by Dollinger, p. 200).

CHAPTER VIII.

RELIGION OF THE ANCIENT ROMANS.

"Sua cuique religio civitati, nostra nobis."
CICERO, *Pro Flacc.* 28.

TIME was, and not a very distant time, when it was regularly inculcated on the youthful mind in our public schools and other great educational establishments, that one and the same religious system prevailed alike in Italy and Greece, among the Romans and the Hellenes; two branches, as it was thought, of a single original people. Such phrases as "classical mythology," "the religion of the Greeks and Romans," "the deities of the classical nations," were frequent alike on the lips of teachers, and in the language of authorized text-books; the Grecian divinities were spoken of almost universally by their (supposed) equivalent Latin names; and the youth would have been considered offensively pedantic who should have hesitated to render "Ηρα by "Juno," or Δημητηρ by "Ceres." But within the last twenty or thirty years a more just appreciation of the facts of the case has sprung up; the careful investigation which has been made of the "origines" both of Greece and Rome has shown,

213

first, that the two nations were but remotely connected in race, and secondly, that their religious systems were markedly and strikingly different. Any review of the religious systems of the ancient world that is attempted at the present day, necessarily and as a matter of course, treats separately the religion of the Hellenes and that of the Romans; and we are thus bound, before our task can be regarded as complete, to append to the account which we have already given of the Hellenic religious system a chapter on the " Religion of the Ancient Romans."

Following the method which we have hitherto for the most part pursued, we propose to consider, first, the objects of worship at Rome, and secondly, the character and peculiarities of the worship which was paid to them. We may note, *en passant*, that the religion was a polytheism, in its general character similar to that of Greece, but distinguished by its comparatively scanty development of the polytheistic idea in respect of Nature and the parts of Nature, and its ample development of that idea in connection with human life, its actions, parts, and phases.

The great gods (*Di majores*) of Rome were always regarded as twelve in number, though at different periods of Roman history the enumeration of " the twelve" would have been different. If we go back to the very earliest—almost pre-historic—time, we may perhaps name the following as " the twelve " of the primitive system—Jupiter, Juno (= Diana), Minerva, Mars, Bellona, Vesta, Ceres, Saturnus,

Ops, Hercules, Mercurius, Neptune. A few words must be said concerning each of these.

JUPITER.

The Jupiter (JV-PATER), or "Father Jove," of the Romans bore a real resemblance to the Greek Zeus, with whose name his is etymologically identical.[1] The idea of paternity, attached to his name in ordinary parlance, implied the same notion which we find in the Hellenic system, viz., that he was "the father of gods and men" (*hominum sator atque deorum*, Virg.). He had a temple from the very earliest times on the Capitoline hill, where he was worshipped in combination with Juno and Minerva, and a High Priest, the "Flamen Dialis," who maintained his cult with perpetual burnt sacrifice. Originally, there must have been in the conception of Jupiter a latent monotheism; but long before the first settlement was made by any Latins in Italy, this idea seems to have evaporated; and to the Romans of the earliest times whereof we have any trace, Jove was no more than one god out of many[2]—the god, especially, of the air, the sky, the firmament—who sent down lightning from above, gave rain, directed the flight of birds, and (as Ve-Jovis) impregnated the atmosphere with fevers and pestilence. He was

[1] Both names are, of course, closely allied to the Sanskrit "Dyaus," "heaven," or "the sky." (See Max Müller, "Science of Religion," p. 172.)

[2] This is applied in the ordinary appendage to his name, "Optimus maximus," "the best and greatest" (of the gods).

the acknowledged head of the Roman pantheon, only preceded sometimes in solemn invocations[1] by Janus, "the spirit of opening," who necessarily presided over beginnings of all kinds. A sort of general superintendence over human affairs was assigned to him; he was viewed as punishing impiety in general, and perjury in particular; he knew the future, and could reveal it; he guarded the rights of property, and was viewed as a sort of guardian deity of the Roman people and state. He has been called, "the genius of the Roman people;"[2] but this conception of him is too narrow. He was certainly much more than that. If not the "universal lord," which some have considered him, he was at any rate a great god —the highest conception of deity which was ever reached by the Romans.

JUNO.

Juno is a mere female Jupiter, possessing no substantive or separate character, unless it be that of a special protectress of women, and more particularly of matrons. She stands to Jupiter as Fauna to Faunus, Luna to Lunus, Amente to Ammon. She presided especially over marriages and births, being invoked as "Lucina," or "she that brings to light," when the birth drew nigh, and as "Pronuba" when marriage approached. Identical with Diana originally (for Diana is to Διος as Juno to Ζευς), she came gradually to be considered a distinct and sepa-

---

[1] Liv. viii. 9.
[2] Mommsen, "History of Rome," vol. i. p. 176, E. T.

rate deity—the distinction becoming a contrast in the later times, when Diana was identified with the Grecian Artemis. As Jupiter was the "king," so Juno was the "queen of heaven" (*regina cœli* or *cœlorum*). She was invoked under many names besides those already mentioned. She was "Virginalis," as protecting maidens; "Matrona," as the patroness of married women; "Opigena," "help-giving;" and "Sospita," "preserving," as general aider of the female sex. A great festival was held in her honour every year on the 1st of March, which was called *Matronalia*, and was attended by all Roman matrons, who regarded her as at her pleasure either giving or withholding offspring. It was perhaps an accident which gave Juno the presidency over money, the Romans having found it convenient to establish their first mint in the vicinity of her temple on the Capitoline hill, where she was worshipped as Juno Moneta, or "Juno the admonitress."

MINERVA.

Minerva, though worshipped in common by the Etruscans and the Romans, appears by the etymology of her name to have been essentially a Latin deity. She is the goddess of mind (*mens*) and memory (*memini*, *reminiscor*)—"the thinking, calculating, inventive power personified."[1] Her worship was closely connected with that of Jupiter and Juno, the three together forming the Capitoline Triad, who

[1] Schmidt, in Dr. Smith's "Dict. of Greek and Roman Antiquities," vol. ii p. 1090.

alone had temples on that hill in the early times. In the great *lectisternium* called *epulum Jovis*, the images of the three were brought out and feasted together. Minerva was the patroness both of the fine arts and of the various handicrafts—the goddess of sculptors, painters, musicians, poets, physicians, weavers, dyers, carpenters, smiths, etc., etc. Each man regarded his talents as coming especially from her; and as success in war is the fruit of prudence, perseverance, contrivance, stratagem, as much as of courage and sheer brute force, Minerva was in one respect[1] a war-goddess, and represented with a helmet, shield, and coat of mail. The chief festival celebrated in honour of Minerva was the Quinquatrus or Quinquatria, which lasted five days—from the 19th of March to the 23rd.

MARS.

In Mavors or Mars we have " the central object, not only of Roman, but Italian, worship in general"[1] —the real main object of public religious regard throughout the greater portion of the peninsula. Originally, perhaps, Maurs (Mors), " the killing god," and therefore, like Siva the Destroyer, attached to no special department of human life, he came by degrees to have the most destructive of human occupations, war, assigned to him as his especial field, and to be regarded as the god who went out to battle at the head of each army—invisibly but really present —who hurled his spear at the foe, struck terror into

[1] So Mommsen, " History of Rome," vol. i. p. 175, E. T.

them, disordered their ranks, and gave to his worshippers the victory. Practically ousting Jupiter
from the regards of men, he became Marspiter[1]
(Maspiter, "Father Mars," *the* god to whom alone
they looked for protection. The first month of the
year was dedicated to him, and thence took the name
which it bears in most modern European languages.
The great muster-ground of the people before they
went out to war became the "Campus Martius;" and
war itself was sometimes designated by his name, as
intellectual ability was by that of Minerva. As
marching at the head of Roman troops, he was
called *Gradivus*, as avenging them upon their
enemies, *Ultor*. Like Jupiter, he had his High
Priest—the "Flamen Martialis"—whose business
it was to present to him burnt offerings. He had
also attached to his worship from very ancient times
a college of priests known as Salii ("dancers"), who
performed war-dances in his honour, clad in armour,
and carrying the sacred shields supposed to have
fallen from heaven, and called *ancilia*. The wolf,
the horse, and the woodpecker were sacred to him.
A great festival was held in his honour at the beginning of each year, commencing on the 1st March.

BELLONA.

Bellona, or Duellona,[2] stood to Mars as Juno to
Jupiter, except that there was no etymological connection between the names. She was the goddess of

---

[1] Liv. viii. 9.
[2] Fabretti, "Corpus Inscr. Italicarum," p. 323.

war (*bellum* or *duellum*), was spoken of as the wife or sister of Mars, and had a temple in the Campus Martius, where the ceremony of proclaiming war was performed. A college of priests, called Bellonarii, conducted her worship, and were bound, when they offered sacrifice in her honour, to wound their own arms or legs, and either to offer up upon her altar the blood which flowed from their wounds, or else to swallow it themselves. The 24th of March was especially appointed for these ceremonies, and for this reason was known in the Roman calendar as the " day of blood " (*dies sanguinis*). Bellona was represented as armed with a bloody scourge,[1] and was solemnly invoked in dangerous crises by generals on the battle field.[2]

VESTA.

Vesta, identical with the Grecian Hestia ('Εστέα), was an ancient goddess, whose worship the Latins brought with them into Italy from their primitive settlements in the far East. In her earliest conception, she was the goddess of the human dwelling (*vas, vasana,* Sanskr.) generally : but, according to Roman ideas, it was the national, rather than the domestic, hearth over which she presided. Her temple was one of the most ancient in Rome. It lay at the northern foot of the Palatine hill, a little east of the Forum, and was in the immediate vicinity of a sacred grove, also dedicated to Vesta. The regular

[1] Virgil, " Æn." viii. 703; Lucan, " Phars." vii. 569.
[2] Liv. viii. 9; x. 19.

worship of the goddess was entrusted to a college of six women, known as "Vestal Virgins" (*Virgines Vestales*), whose special duty it was to preserve the sacred fire upon the altar which represented the national hearthstone, and not to allow it ever to be extinguished. They dwelt together in a cloister (*atrium*) a little apart from the temple, under the presidency of the eldest sister (*Vestalis maxima*) and under the superintendence and control of the college of Pontifices. Besides watching the fire, they had to present offerings to Vesta at stated times, and to sprinkle and purify the shrine each morning with water from the Egerian spring. A festival was held in honour of the goddess annually on the 9th of June, at which no man might be present, but which was attended by the Roman matrons generally, who walked in procession with bare feet from the various quarters of the city to the temple. There was no image in the temple of Vesta, the eternal fire being regarded as symbolising her sufficiently.

CERES.

A god, Cerus, and a goddess Ceric, are found to have been worshipped by the early Italians;[1] and it is a reasonable conjecture that these names are connected with the Latin "Ceres." The Latin writers derived that word either from *gero* or *creo*,[2] and con-

---

[1] Fabretti, "Corpus Ins. Italic." pp. 829, 830.

[2] Varro ("De Ling. Lat." v. 64), and Cicero ("De Nat. Deor." ii. 26), derive it from *gero;* Servius ("Comm. ad Virg. Georg." i. 6), and Macrobius ("Saturn." i. 18) from *creo.*

sidered that it was given to mark that the deity in question was the "bringer " or "creator" of those fruits of the earth on which the life of man mainly depends. According to some, Ceres was the same as Tellus ; but this does not seem to have been the case anciently. Ceres was the goddess of agriculture, and was connected from a very early date with Liber, the Latin Bacchus, the god of the vineyard. That Ceres should have been one of the "great divinities," marks strongly the agricultural character of the early Roman state, which did not give to Liber, or to Pomona, any such position. The worship of Ceres merged after a time in that of Demeter, whose peculiar rites were imported either from Velia or from Sicily.

SATURNUS.

Saturnus was properly the god of sowing, but was regarded, like Ceres, as a general deity of agriculture, and was represented with a pruning-hook in his hand, and with wool about his feet. His statue was made hollow, and was filled with olive oil, significant of the "fatness" and fertility which he spread over the land. His festival, the Saturnalia, held in December, from the 17th to the 24th, was a sort of harvest-home, commemorative of the conclusion of all the labours of the year, and was therefore celebrated with jocund rites, mirth, and festivity, an intermixture of all ranks upon equal terms, and an interchange of presents. The temple of Saturn at Rome stood at the foot of the Capitoline hill, and was assigned to a remote antiquity, though with variations as to the exact date. It was used as a record office, and also as the public treasury, which was regarded as mainly filled by the produce of agricultural industry. The identification of Saturnus with the Grecian Cronus was a foolish fancy of the Hellenising period, the truth being that "there is no resemblance whatever between the attributes of the two deities."[1]

OPS.

With Saturn must be placed Ops, who was sometimes called his wife, and whose worship certainly stood in a very close connection with his. Ops was properly the divinity of field-labour (*opus, opera*); but as such labour is productive of wealth, Ops came to be also the goddess of plenty and of riches, and her name is the root-element in such words as *opimus, opulentus, inops*, and the like. She was generally worshipped together with Saturn, and had temples in common with him; but still she had her own separate sanctuary on the Capitoline hill,[2] where honours were paid to her apart from any other deity. Her festival, the Opalia, fell on December 19th, or the third day of the Saturnalia, and was thus practically merged in that of the god of agriculture. Ops, like Ceres, is sometimes confounded with Tellus, but the three goddesses were to the Latin mind distinct, Tellus being a personification of the earth itself, Ceres of the productive power in nature, which brings forth fruits

[1] Schmidt, in Smith's "Dict. of Greek and Roman Biog." vol. iii. p. 726.
[2] Liv. xxxix. 22.

out of the earth, and Ops of the human labour without which the productive power runs to waste, and is insufficient for the sustenance of human life.

HERCULES.

The near resemblance of Hercules to Heracles led, almost necessarily, to the idea, everywhere prevalent until recently, that the two gods were identical, and that therefore either Hercules was an ancient deity common to the Latins with the Hellenes before the former migrated into Italy, or else that he was an importation from Greece, introduced at a comparatively late period. Recently, however, the etymological connection of the two names has been questioned, and it has been suggested[1] that Hercules is, like Ceres, and Saturn, and Ops, and Mars, and Minerva, a genuine Italic god, quite unconnected with Heracles, who is a genuine Hellenic divinity. The root of the name Hercules has been found in *hercus* (ἕρκος) "a fence" or "enclosure," whence *hercere* or *arcere*, "to ward off," "keep back," "shield." Hercules, whose worship was certainly as ancient at Rome as that of any other deity, would thus be "the god of the enclosed homestead," and thence in general "the god of property and gain."[2] He was regarded as presiding over faith, the basis of the social contract, and of all dealings between man and man, and hence was known as *Deus fidius,* "the god of good faith," who avenged infractions of it. In

---

[1] Mommsen, "History of Rome," vol. i. p. 174.
[2] *Ibid.*

the early times he seems to have had no temple at
Rome; but his Great Altar in the cattle-market was
one of the most sacred sites in the city;[1] oaths were
sworn there, and contracts concluded; nor was it
unusual for Roman citizens to devote to it a tenth
part of their property, for the purpose of obtaining
the god's favour, or for the fulfilment of a vow.
The worship of Hercules was not exclusively Roman,
not even Latin, but Italic. He was "reverenced in
every spot of Italy, and had altars erected to him
everywhere, in the streets of the towns as well as by
the roadsides."[2]

MERCURIUS.

Mercurius was the god of commerce and traffic
generally. As trade was not looked upon with much
respect at Rome, his position among the "great gods"
was a low one. He had no very ancient temple or
priesthood, and, when allowed the honour of a temple in the second decade of the Republic,[3] his worship seems to have been regarded as plebeian and of
an inferior character. Connected with it was a
"guild of merchants"[4] (*collegium mercatorum*), called
afterwards, "Mercuriales," who met at the temple
on certain fixed days for a religious purpose. The
cult of Mercury was, like that of Hercules, very
widely diffused; but it was affected chiefly by the
lower orders, and had not much hold upon the
nation.

[1] See Liv. i. 7; ix. 29. [2] Mommsen, l. s. c.
[3] Liv. ii. 27.
[4] Niebuhr, "History of Rome," vol. i. p. 589, note, E. T.

15

NEPTUNUS.

The Latin Neptunus is reasonably identified with the Etruscan Nethuns,[1] who was a water god, widely worshipped by that seafaring people. The word is probably to be connected with the root *nib* or *nip*, found in νίπτω, νιπτήρ, χέρ-νιβ-α, κ. τ. λ. There is not much trace of the worship of Neptune at Rome in the early times, for Livy's identification of him with Consus,[2] the god honoured in the Consualia, cannot be allowed. We find his cult, however, fully established in the second century of the Republic,[3] when it was united with that of Mercury, the mercantile deity. In later times he had an altar in the Circus Flaminius, and a temple in the Campus Martius. A festival was held in his honour, called Neptunalia, on the 23rd day of July, which was celebrated with games, banquets, and carousals. The people made themselves booths at this time with the branches of trees, and feasted beneath the pleasant shade of the green foliage. Roman admirals, on quitting port with a fleet, were bound to sacrifice to Neptune, and the entrails of the victims were thrown into the sea. After the Greek mythology became known to the Romans, Neptune was completely identified with Poseidon, and became invested with all his attributes. Amphitrite became his wife, and the Nereids his companions.[4]

In succession to the twelve deities of the first rank

[1] Taylor, "Etruscan Researches," p. 138.
[2] Liv. i. 9.   [3] *Ibid.* v. 13.   [4] Hor. Od. iii. 28, 1. 10.

may be placed the following important groups:—
1. The gods of the country: Tellus, or Mother Earth; Silvanus, god of the woods; Pomona, goddess of orchards; Flora, goddess of flowers; Faunus ("favouring god"), presiding over flocks and herds; and Vertumnus, god of the changing year (*verto*). 2. The State gods: Terminus, god of the boundary; Consus, god of the State's secret counsels; Quirinus, god of the Quirinal and of the Quirites, or Roman people; and the Penates, gods of the State's property (*penus*). 3. The personifications of abstract qualities: Pietas, goddess of piety; Fides, of faith; Spes, of hope; Pax, of peace abroad; Concordia, of peace at home; Libertas, of liberty; Fortuna, of good luck; Juventas, of youth; Salus, of health; Pudicitia, of modesty; Victoria, of victory; Cupid, god of desire; Pavor, of fright; Pallor, of paleness; and the like. 4. The Nature gods: Coelus, Terra, Sol, Lunus, or Luna, Æsculanus, Argentinus, etc. And 5. The divinities introduced from Greece: Apollo, Bacchus, Latona, Pluto, Plutus, Proserpine, Castor, Pollux, Æsculapius, Priapus, Æolus, the Fates, the Furies, etc.

To this brief sketch of the chief objects of worship among the ancient Romans, it follows to add some account of the character of the worship itself.

The worship of most of the gods was specially provided for by the State, which established paid priesthoods, to secure the continual rendering of the honours due to each. The highest order of priests bore the name of Flamines, which is thought to

The Religions of the Ancient World.

mean "kindlers of fire,"[1] *i.e.*, offerers of burnt sacrifice. The Flamines were of two classes, Majores and Minores, the former of whom were always taken from the patrician order. These were the Flamen Dialis, or "priest of Jove," the Flamen Martialis, or "priest of Mars," and the Flamen Quirinalis, or "priest of Quirinus." Among the Flamines Minores, many of whom were of late institution, we find those of Vertumnus, Flora, Pomona, and Vulcan.[2] The Flamen was in each case the principal sacrificing priest in the chief temple of the god or goddess, and was bound to be in continual attendance upon the shrine, and to superintend the entire worship offered at it. In addition to the Flamen, or in his place, there was attached to all temples a collegium, or body of priests, which might consist of all the male members of a particular family, as the Potitii and Pinarii,[3] but was more commonly a close corporation, limited in number, and elected by co-optation, *i.e.*, by the votes of the existing members.

Amongst the most important of these corporations were the two collegia of Salii, or "dancing priests," which were attached to the temple of Mars upon the Palatine hill, and to that of Quirinus upon the Quirinal. The former—Salii Palatini—had the charge of the ancilia, or sacred shields, one of which was believed to have fallen from heaven, and to be fatally connected with the safety of the Roman State. In the great festival of Mars, with which the year

[1] Mommsen, "History of Rome," vol. i. p. 175.

[2] Ennius ap. Varronem, "De Ling. Lat." vii. 44.   [3] Liv. i. 7.

opened, they marched in procession through the city, bearing the ancilia on their shoulders, and striking them from time to time, as they danced and sang, with a rod. The Salii of Quirinus—Salii Collini or Agonales—were a less important college. Their duties connected them with the worship of Quirinus, who is believed by some to have been the Sabine Mars,[1] and with the festival of the Quirinalia. Like the other Salii, they no doubt performed war-dances in honour of their patron deity. A third collegium, or priestly corporation of high rank, was that of the six Vestal Virgins, attached, as their name implies, to the worship of Vesta, and regarded with peculiar veneration, as having vowed themselves to chastity in the service of the nation. Other collegia of some importance, but of a lower rank, were that of the Fratres Arvales, a college of twelve priests attached to the cult of Ceres, who celebrated a festival to her as the Dea dia (divine goddess) in the early summer time; and that of the Luperci, or "wolf-expellers," a shifting body of persons, whose chief business it was to conduct the Lupercalia, a festival held annually on the 15th of February, in honour of Lupercus, or Faunus. The Sodales Titii had duties similar to those of the Fratres Arvales; and the Flamines Curiales, thirty in number, offered sacrifices for the preservation of the thirty curies of the original Roman people.

From these collegia of priests, we must carefully distinguish the learned corporations, "colleges of

[1] Mommsen, vol. i. pp. 87 and 175.

sacred lore," as they have been called,[1] who had no
priestly duties, and no special connection with any
particular deity. There were four principal colleges
of this kind—those of the Pontifices, the Augurs, the
Fetials, and the Duumviri sacrorum.

The Pontifices, originally four (or five, if we include the pontifex maximus), but afterwards raised to
nine, and ultimately to sixteen, had the general
superintendence of religion. They exercised a control over all the priests, even the Flamens. They
were supposed to be thoroughly acquainted with all
the traditions with regard to the appropriate worship
of each divinity; to understand the mysteries of num-
bers, and to be deeply versed in astronomy—whence
they settled the calendar, determining when each
festival was to be held, and what days were *fasti* or
nefasti, i.e., days suitable for the transaction of business, or the contrary. All prodigies and omens had
to be reported to them; and with them it lay to determine what steps should be taken to appease the
gods in connection with each. They had to furnish
the proper formula on all great religious occasions, as
the dedication of a temple,[2] the self-devotion of a
general,[3] and the like. There was no appeal from
their decisions, unless in some cases to the people;
and they could enforce obedience by the infliction of
fines, and, under certain circumstances, of death.

The Augurs, originally four, like the Pontiffs, and
raised, like them, first to nine, and later to sixteen,

[1] Mommsen, vol. i. p. 177, 178.
[2] Liv. i. 46.　　　[3] *Ibid.* viii. 9; x. 28.

were regarded as possessed especially of the sacred
lore connected with birds. Augural birds were limited
in number, and were believed to give omens in three
ways, by flight, by note, or by manner of feeding.
The Augurs knew exactly what constituted a good,
and what a bad, omen in all these ways. They were
consulted whenever the State commenced any important business. No assembly could be held, no
election could take place, no war could be begun, no
consul could quit Rome, no site for a new temple
could be fixed on, unless the Augurs were present,
and pronounced that the birds gave favourable omens.
In war, they watched the feeding of the sacred
chickens, and allowed or forbade engagements, according as the birds ate greedily or the contrary.
Divination from celestial phenomena, especially
thunder and lightning, was, at a comparatively late
date, added to their earlier functions. As their
duties enabled them to exercise a veto upon laws,
and very seriously to influence elections, the office
was much sought after by candidates for political
power, and was regarded as one of the highest digni-
ties in the State.[1]

The Fetials, a college of (probably) twenty persons, were the living depositary of international law
and right. All the treaty obligations of Rome and
her neighbours were supposed to be known to them,
and it was for them to determine when a war could
be justly undertaken, and what reparation should be
demanded for injuries. Not only did they furnish

[1] Cic. De Leg. ii. 12.

the forms for demanding satisfaction,[1] declaring war,[2] and making peace,[3] but their own personal intervention was requisite in every case. Invested with a sacred character, they were the intermediaries employed by the State in making complaints, proclaiming war, and seeing that treaties were concluded with the proper formalities. In the conclusion of such engagements they even acted as veritable priests, slaying with their own hands the victims, by offering which a sacred character was given to treaty obligations.

The Duumviri sacrorum were the keepers, consulters, and interpreters of the Sibylline books, a collection of pretended prophecies, written in Greek, and no doubt derived from a Greek source. They were, as their name implies, a collegium of two persons only,[4] and in the early times were required to be Romans of a very high rank. As such persons, not unfrequently, were very ignorant of the Greek, the State furnished them with two slaves well acquainted with the language. It was customary to consult the Sibyline books in case of pestilence, or of any extraordinary prodigy, and to follow scrupulously the advice which they were thought to give in reference to the occasion.

Such were the learned colleges of ancient Rome. Though exercising considerable political influence, they never became dangerous to the State, from the

[1] Liv. i. 32.   [2] *Ibid.*   [3] *Ibid.* i. 24.
[4] The office was subsequently expanded into that of the decemviri sacris faciundis, who ultimately became quindecimviri.

circumstance that they could in no case take the initiative. Their business was to give answers to inquirers; and, until consulted, they were dumb. Private persons as well as public officers might appeal to them; and calls were frequently made on them to bring forth their secret knowledge into the light of day by the magistrates. But it was of their essence to be consultative, and not initiative, or even executive bodies. Hence, notwithstanding the powers which they wielded, and the respect in which they were held, they at no time became a danger to the State. Sacerdotalism plays no part in Roman history. "Notwithstanding all their zeal for religion, the Romans adhered with unbending strictness to the principle, that the priest ought to remain completely powerless in the State, and, excluded from command, ought, like any other burgess, to render obedience to the humblest magistrate." [1]

The public religion of the Romans consisted, mainly, in the observance by the State of its obligation (*religio*) to provide for the cult of certain traditional deities, which it did by building temples, establishing priesthoods, and securing the continuance of both by endowments. Further, the State showed a constant sense of religion by the position which it assigned to augury, and the continual need of "taking the auspices" on all important civil occasions. In declaring war, religious formulæ were used; in conducting it, the augurs, or their subordinates, were frequently consulted; in bringing it to

[1] Mommsen, "History of Rome," vol. i. p. 180.

an end and establishing peace, the fetials had to be called in, and the sanction of religion thus secured to each pacific arrangement. The great officers of the State were inducted into their posts with religious solemnities, and were bound to attend and take their part in certain processions and sacrifices. In times of danger and difficulty the State gave orders for special religious ceremonies, to secure the favour of the gods, or avert their wrath.

The religion of the mass of the people consisted principally in four things: 1. Daily offerings by each head of a household (*paterfamilias*) to the Lares of his own house. The Lares were viewed as household gods, who watched over each man's hearth and home, each house having its own special Lares. In theory they were the spirits of ancestors, and their chief, the Lar familiaris, was the spirit of the first ancestor, the originator of the family; but practically the ancestral idea was not prominent. In respectable houses there was always a lararium,[1] or "lar-chapel," containing the images of the Lares; and each religious Roman commenced the day with prayer in this place, accompanying his prayer, upon most occasions, with offerings, which were placed before the images in little dishes (*patellæ*). The offerings were continually renewed at meal-times; and on birthdays and other days of rejoicing the images were adorned

---

[1] The Emperor Alexander Severus had two lararia, and included amongst the Lares of the one, Abraham, Orpheus, Alexander the Great, and Christ; amongst those of the other, Achilles, Cicero, and Virgil.

with wreaths, and the lararia were thrown open. 2. Occasional thank-offerings to particular gods from persons who thought they had been favoured by them. These were carried to the temples by the donors, and made over to the priests, who formally offered them, with an accompaniment of hymns and prayers. 3. Vows and their performance. To obtain a particular favour from a god supposed to be capable of granting it, a Roman was accustomed to utter a vow, by which he bound himself to make the god a certain present, in case he obtained his desire. The present might be a temple, or an altar, or a statue, or a vase, or any other work of art, but was almost always something of a permanent character. The Roman, having made his vow, and got his wish, was excessively scrupulous in the discharge of his obligation, which he viewed as of the most binding character. 4. Attendance at religious festivals—the Carmentalia, Cerealia, Compitalia, Consualia, Floralia, Lemuralia, Lupercalia, etc. This attendance was in no sense obligatory, and was viewed rather as pleasure than duty—the festivals being usually celebrated with games (*ludi*) and other amusements.

Upon the whole, the Roman religion, as compared with others, and especially with that of the Greeks, strikes us as dull, tame, and matter-of-fact. There is no beauty in it, no play of the imagination, and very little mystery. It is "of earth, earthy." Its gods are not great enough, or powerful enough, to impress the mind of the worshipper with a perma-

nent sense of religious awe—they do not force the
soul to bow down before them in humility and self-
abasement. The Roman believes in gods, admits
that he receives benefits from them, allows the duty
of gratitude, and, as a just man, punctually dis-
charges the obligations of his religion.[1] But his
creed is not elevating—it does not draw him on to
another world—it does not raise in him any hopes of
the future. Like the Sadducee, he thinks that God
rewards and punishes men, as He does nations, in this
life; his thoughts rarely turn to another; and if they
do, it is with a sort of shiver at the prospect of becoming a pale shade, haunting the neighbourhood of
the tomb, or dwelling in the cold world beneath, shut
out from the light of day.

If the Roman religion may be said to have had
anywhere a deeper character than this—to have been
mysterious, soul-stirring, awful—it was in connection
with the doctrine of expiation. In the bright clime
of Italy, and in the strong and flourishing Roman
community, intensely conscious of its own life and
vigour, the gods could not but be regarded predominantly as beneficent beings, who showered blessings
upon mankind. But occasionally, under special
circumstances, a different feeling arose. Earth-
quakes shook the city, and left great yawning gaps
in its streets or squares; the Tiber overflowed its
banks, and inundated all the low regions that lay
about the Seven Hills; pestilence broke out, destroy-

[1] Note the idea of obligation as predominant in the word
"religion," from *re* and *lego* or *ligo*, "to bind" or "tie."

ing thousands, and threatening to carry off the entire people; or the fortune of war hung in suspense, nay, even turned against the warrior nation. At such times a sense of guilt arose, and pressed heavily on the consciences of the Romans; they could not doubt that Heaven was angry with them; they did not dare to dispute that the Divine wrath was provoked by their sins. Then sacrifice, which in Rome was generally mere thank-offering, took the character of atonement or expiation. The gods were felt to require a victim, or victims; and something must be found to content them—something of the best and dearest that the State possessed. What could this be but a human sacrifice? Such a sacrifice might be either voluntary or involuntary. Enhanced by the noble quality of patriotic self-abnegation, a single victim sufficed—more especially if he were of the best and noblest—a young patrician of high promise, like Marcus Curtius,[1] or an actual consul, like the Decii.[2] Without this quality there must be several victims—either a sacred and complete number, like the thirty, once offered annually at the Lemuralia, whereof the thirty rush dolls thrown yearly into the Tiber were a reminiscence, or else an indefinite number, such as the gods themselves might determine on, as when a " ver sacrum " was proclaimed, and all offspring, both of men and of sacrificial cattle, produced within the first month of opening spring

[1] Liv. vii. 6.
[2] *Ibid.* vii. 9; x. 28.

(Aprilis), were devoted to death and sacrificed to avert God's wrath from the nation.[1]

The mythological fables in which the Greeks indulged from a very early date were foreign to the spirit of the Romans, who had no turn for allegory, and regarded the gods with too much respect and fear to invent tales about them. No traditional accounts of the dealings of the gods one with another gave a divine sanction to immorality, or prevented the Romans from looking up to their divinities as at once greater and better than themselves. The moral law was recognised as an accepted standard with them, and its vindication whenever it was transgressed rested with the deity within whose special sphere the offence was conceived to fall. Hercules avenged broken faith; Ops and Ceres punished the lazy cultivator; ill-conducted matrons incurred the anger of Juno; the violation of parental or filial duty fell under the cognisance of Jupiter. Whenever conduct was felt to be wrong, yet the civil law visited the misconduct with no penalty, the displeasure of the gods supplemented the legal defect, and caused the offender in course of time to meet with due punishment. Their belief on this head was, in part, the effect, but it was also, in part, the cause of those profound moral convictions which distinguished the Romans among ancient nations. They were deeply impressed with the reality of moral distinctions, and convinced that sin was in all cases followed by suffer-

---

[1] See Festus, *sub voc.* "Ver sacrum," and compare Liv. xxiii. 9, 10; xxxiv. 44; Servius ad Virg. Æn. vii. 796, etc.

ing. The stings of conscience received increased force and power from the belief in a Divine agency that seconded the judgments of conscience, and never failed to punish offenders.[1]

It is not the object of the present work to trace the changes which came in course of time over the Roman religion, or even to note the corrupting influences to which it was exposed. The subject of "Ancient Religions" is so large a one, that we have felt compelled to limit ourselves in each of our portraitures to the presentation of the religion in a single aspect, that, namely, which it wore at the full completion of its natural and national development. To do more, to trace each religion historically from its first appearance to its last phase, would require as many chapters as we have had pages at our disposal. The influence of religions upon each other is a matter of so much difficulty, delicacy, and occasional complexity, that it would necessitate discussions of very considerable length. An exhaustive work on the history of religions would have to embrace this ample field, and must necessarily run to several volumes. In the present series of sketches, limited as we have been as to space, we have attempted no more than the fringe of a great subject, and have sought to awaken the curiosity of our readers rather than to satisfy it.

---

[1] Hor. Od. iii. 2, ll. 31, 32 ; Tibull. Carm. i. 9, l. 4.

CONCLUDING REMARKS.

It has been maintained in the "Introduction" to this work, that the time is not yet come for the construction of a "Science of Religion," and that the present need is rather to accumulate materials, out of which ultimately such a science may perhaps be evolved. Still, the accumulation of materials naturally suggests certain thoughts of a more general character; and the spirit of the Baconian philosophy does not forbid the drawing of inferences from groups of phenomena, even while the greater portion of the phenomena are unknown or uninvestigated. While, therefore, we abstain from basing any positive theory upon a survey of religions which is confessedly incomplete, we think that certain negative conclusions of no little interest may be drawn even from the data now before us; and these negative conclusions it seems to be our duty to lay before the reader, at any rate for his consideration.

In the first place, it seems impossible to trace back to any one fundamental conception, to any innate idea, or to any common experience or observation, the various religions which we have been considering. The veiled monotheism of Egypt, the dualism of Persia, the shamanism of Etruria, the pronounced
240

polytheism of India, are too contrariant, too absolutely unlike, to admit of any one explanation, or to be derivatives from a single source. The human mind craves unity; but Nature is wonderfully complex. The phenomena of ancient religions, so far as they have been investigated, favour the view that religions had not one origin, but several distinct origins.

Secondly, it is clear that from none of the religions here treated of could the religion of the ancient Hebrews have originated. The Israelite people at different periods of its history came, and remained for a considerable time, under Egyptian, Babylonian, and Persian influence; and there have not been wanting persons of ability who have regarded "Judaism" as a mere offshoot from the religion of one or other of these three peoples. But, with the knowledge that we have now obtained of the religions in question, such views have been rendered untenable, if not henceforth impossible. Judaism stands out from all other ancient religions, as a thing *sui generis*, offering the sharpest contrast to the systems prevalent in the rest of the East, and so entirely different from them in its spirit and its essence that its origin could not but have been distinct and separate.

Thirdly, the sacred Books of the Hebrews cannot possibly have been derived from the sacred writings of any of these nations. No contrast can be greater than that between the Pentateuch and the "Ritual of the Dead," unless it be that between the Pentateuch and the Zendavesta, or between the same work and the Vedas. A superficial resemblance may perhaps

16

be traced between portions of the Pentateuch and certain of the myths of ancient Babylon ; but the tone and spirit of the two are so markedly different, that neither can be regarded as the original of the other. Where they approach most nearly, as in the accounts given of the Deluge, while the facts recorded are the same, or nearly the same, the religious stand-point is utterly unlike.[1]

Fourthly, the historic review which has been here made lends no support to the theory, that there is a uniform growth and progress of religions from fetishism to polytheism, from polytheism to monotheism, and from monotheism to positivism, as maintained by the followers of Comte. None of the religions here described shows any signs of having been developed out of fetishism, unless it be the shamanism of the Etruscans. In most of them the monotheistic idea is most prominent *at the first*, and gradually becomes obscured, and gives way before a polytheistic corruption. In all there is one element, at least, which appears to be traditional, viz., sacrifice, for it can scarcely have been by the exercise of his reason that man came so generally to believe that the superior powers, whatever they were, would be pleased by the violent death of one or more of their creatures.

Altogether, the theory to which the facts appear on the whole to point, is the existence of a primitive religion, communicated to man from without, where-

---

[1] Compare above, pp. 68–72 ; and see the Author's Essay in "Aids to Faith." Essay vi., pp. 275, 276.

of monotheism and expiatory sacrifice were parts, and
the gradual clouding over of this primitive revelation everywhere, unless it were among the Hebrews.
Even among them a worship of Teraphim crept in
(Gen. xxxi. 19–35), together with other corruptions
(Josh. xxiv. 14); and the terrors of Sinai were
needed to clear away polytheistic accretions. Elsewhere degeneration had free play. "A dark cloud
stole over man's original consciousness of the
Divinity; and, in consequence of his own guilt, an
estrangement of the creature from the one living
God took place; man, as under the overpowering
sway of sense and sensual lust, proportionally
weakened, therefore, in his moral freedom, was unable any longer to conceive of the Divinity as a
pure, spiritual, supernatural, and infinite Being, distinct from the world, and exalted above it. And
thus it followed, inevitably, that, with his intellectual
horizon bounded and confined within the limits of
nature, he should seek to satisfy the inborn necessity
of an acknowledgment and reverence of the Divinity
by the deification of material nature ; for even in its
obscuration, the idea of the Deity, no longer recognised, indeed, but still felt and perceived, continued
powerful; and, in conjunction with it, the truth struck
home, that the Divinity manifested itself in nature
as ever present and in operation."[1] The cloud was
darker and thicker in some places than in others.
There were, perhaps, races with whom the whole of
the past became a *tabula rasa*, and all traditional

[1] Dollinger, "Jew and Gentile," vol. i. p. 65.

knowledge being lost, religion was evolved afresh out of the inner consciousness. There were others which lost a portion, without losing the whole of their inherited knowledge. There were others again who lost scarcely anything ; but hid up the truth in mystic language and strange symbolism. The only theory which accounts for all the facts—for the unity as well as the diversity of Ancient Religions, is that of a primeval revelation, variously corrupted through the manifold and multiform deterioration of human nature in different races and places.

INDEX.

245

The Origin and Growth of Religion, as Illustrated by

THE RELIGION OF
ANCIENT EGYPT.

By P. LE PAGE RENOUF.

(The Hibbert Lectures for 1879.)

One volume, 12mo, - - - - - - - $1.50

M. Le Page Renouf's great reputation as an Egyptologist led to his selection to deliver the second course of the already celebrated Hibbert series. His lectures are the fit companions of Professor Muller's, both in learning and in interest. The glimpses laboriously gained by the aid of long undeciphered hieroglyphics into one of the most mystical and profound of all the ancient beliefs, have always had a special fascination ; and the time has now come when it is possible to join their results into a fairly complete picture. Done as this is by M. Renouf, with a certain French vividness and clearness, it has a very unusual, and, indeed, unique interest.

CRITICAL NOTICES.

" The narrative is so well put together, the chain of reasoning and inference so obvious, and the illustration so apt, that the general reader can go through it with unabated interest."—*Hartford Post.*

" No one can rise from reading this book, in which, by the way, the author is careful about drawing his conclusions, without having increased respect for the religion of ancient Egypt, and hardly less than admiration for its ethical system."—*The Churchman.*

" These lectures are invaluable to students of Egyptology, and as the religion of ancient Egypt stands alone and unconnected with other religions, except those which have been modified by it, itself being apparently original and underived, they should be highly interesting to all students of religious history. . . . It is impossible in a brief notice to convey an adequate idea of Professor Renouf's admirable lectures."—*N. Y. World.*

" The present work forms a remarkably intelligent and acutely critical contribution to the history of the origin and growth of religion, as illustrated by the religion of ancient Egypt. As a specialist, Professor Renouf is able to bring forth much information not ordinarily accessible to the general reader, and this he does in such a carefully digested form as to make the work entertaining and instructive in the highest degree."—*Boston Courier.*

*** For sale by all booksellers, or sent, post-paid, upon receipt of price, by

CHARLES SCRIBNER'S SONS, Publishers,
743 and 745 Broadway, New York.

RELIGION AND CHEMISTRY.

By Prof. JOSIAH P. COOKE,

OF HARVARD UNIVERSITY.

A New Edition, with Additions.

One Volume, 12mo, ... $1.50.

The facts of astronomy, as they have been revealed by a long line of splendid discoveries, have already been applied many times to the argument of design in nature; Professor Cooke here applies to it the hardly less wonderful facts of chemistry.

The Conflicts of the Age.

One Vol., 8vo,   -   Paper, 50 Cts. ; Cloth, 75 Cts.

The four articles which make up this little volume are :

(1) An Advertisement for a New Religion.   By an Evolutionist.
(2) The Confession of an Agnostic.   By an Agnostic.
(3) What Morality have we left ?   By a New-Light Moralist.
(4) Review of the Fight.   By a Yankee Farmer.

The secret of its authorship has not yet transpired, and the reviewers seem badly puzzled in their attempts to solve the mystery.

CRITICAL NOTICES.

" Nowhere can an ordinary reader see in a more simple and pleasing form the absurdities which he in the modern speculations about truth and duty. We have no key to the authorship, but the writer evidently holds a practiced pen, and knows how to give that air of *persiflage* in treating of serious subjects which sometimes is more effective than the most cogent dialectic."—*Christian Intelligencer.*

" It is the keenest, best sustained exposure of the weaknesses inherent in certain schools of modern thought, which we have yet come across, and is couched in a vein of fine satire, making it exceedingly readable.   For an insight into the systems it touches upon, and for its suggestions of methods of meeting them, it is capable of being a great help to the clergy.   It is a new departure in apologetics, quite in the spirit of the time."— *The Living Church.*

" The writer has chosen to appear anonymously ; but he holds a pen keen as a Damascus blade.   Indeed, there are few men living capable of writing these papers, and of dissecting so thoroughly the popular conceits and shams of the day.   It is done, too, with a coolness, self-possession, and *sang-froid*, that are inimitable, however uncomfortable it may seem to the writhing victims."—*The Guardian.*

" These four papers are unqualifiedly good.   They show a thorough acquaintance with the whole range of philosophic thought in its modern phases of development, even down to the latest involutions and convolutions of the Evolutionists, the sage unknowableness of the Agnostic, and the New Light novelty of Ethics without a conscience."— *Lutheran Church Review.*

" These papers are as able as they are readable, and are not offensive in their spirit, beyond the necessary offensiveness of belief to the believing mind."—*N. Y. Christian Advocate.*

" The discussion is sprightly, incisive, and witty ; and whoever begins to read it will be likely to read it through."—*New Englander.*

** For   sale   by   all   booksellers,   or   sent,   postpaid,   upon   receipt   of price, by

CHARLES SCRIBNER'S SONS, PUBLISHERS,

743 AND 745 BROADWAY, NEW YORK.

The

Conflict of Christianity

WITH HEATHENISM.

By DR. GERHARD UHLHORN.

TRANSLATED BY

PROF. EGBERT C. SMYTH and REV. C. J. H. ROPES.

One Volume, Crown 8vo, $2.50.

This volume describes with extraordinary vividness and spirit the religious and moral condition of the Pagan world, the rise and spread of Christianity, its conflict with heathenism, and its final victory. There is no work that portrays the heroic age of the ancient church with equal spirit, elegance, and incisive power. The author has made thorough and independent study both of the early Christian literature and also of the contemporary records of classic heathenism.

CRITICAL NOTICES.

"It is easy to see why this volume is so highly esteemed. It is systematic, thorough, and concise. But its power is in the wide mental vision and well-balanced imagination of the author, which enable him to reconstruct the scenes of ancient history. An exceptional clearness and force mark his style."—*Boston Advertiser.*

"One might read many books without obtaining more than a fraction of the profitable information here conveyed ; and he might search a long time before finding one which would so thoroughly fix his attention and command his interest."—*Phil. S. S. Times.*

"Dr. Uhlhorn has described the great conflict with the power of a master. His style is strong and attractive, his descriptions vivid and graphic, his illustrations highly colored, and his presentation of the subject earnest and effective."—*Providence Journal.*

"The work is marked for its broad humanitarian views, its learning, and the wide discretion in selecting from the great field the points of deepest interest."—*Chicago Inter-Ocean.*

"This is one of those clear, strong, thorough-going books which are a scholar's delight."—*Hartford Religious Herald.*

⁎⁎⁎ For sale by all booksellers, or sent post-paid upon receipt of price, by

CHARLES SCRIBNER'S SONS,

Nos. 743 and 745 Broadway, New York.

THE ORIGIN OF NATIONS

By Professor GEORGE RAWLINSON, M.A.

One Volume, 12mo. With maps, . . . *$1.00.*

The first part of this book, Early Civilizations, discusses the antiquity of civilization in Egypt and the other early nations of the East. The second part, Ethnic Affinities in the Ancient World, is an examination of the ethnology of Genesis, showing its accordance with the latest results of modern ethnographical science.

"An attractive volume, which is well worthy of the careful consideration of every reader."—*Observer.*

"A work of genuine scholarly excellence, and a useful offset to a great deal of the superficial current literature on such subjects."—*Congregationalist.*

"Dr. Rawlinson brings to this discussion long and patient research, a vast knowledge and intimate acquaintance with what has been written on both sides of the question."—
Brooklyn Union-Argus.

THE DAWN OF HISTORY.

AN INTRODUCTION TO PRE-HISTORIC STUDY.

Edited by C. F. KEARY, M. A.,
OF THE BRITISH MUSEUM.

One Volume, 12mo., - - - $1.25.

This work treats successively of the earliest traces of man in the remains discovered in caves or elsewhere in different parts of Europe ; of language, its growth, and the story it tells of the pre-historic users of it ; of the races of mankind, early social life, the religions, mythologies, and folk-tales of mankind, and of the history of writing. A list of authorities is appended, and an index has been prepared specially for this edition.

"The book may be heartily recommended as probably the most satisfactory summary of the subject that there is."—*Nation.*

"A fascinating manual, without a vestige of the dullness usually charged against scientific works. . . . In its way, the work is a model of what a popular scientific work should be ; it is readable, it is easily understood, and its style is simple, yet dignified, avoiding equally the affectation of the nursery and of the laboratory."—
Boston Sat. Eve. Gazette.

*** *For sale by all booksellers, or sent, post-paid, upon receipt of price, by*

CHARLES SCRIBNER'S SONS, PUBLISHERS,
743 AND 745 BROADWAY, NEW YORK.

Date Due

3640867R00152

Printed in Great Britain
by Amazon.co.uk, Ltd.,
Marston Gate.